Jesus
Laughed

More Praise for Jesus Laughed:

"As I was reading Robert Darden's insightful historical analysis of holy laughter, I caught a glimpse of Mike Yaconelli dancing in heaven with a twinkle in his eye and a rubber chicken on his head. I know 'Jesus laughed' and rescued me from many a dark night of the soul, for Mike and Robert taught me so."
—Becky Garrison, author of *The New Atheist Crusaders and Their Unholy Grail* and *Red and Blue God, Black and Blue Church*

"Who knew there was so much humor in the Bible? Bob Darden gives us a witty tour through the Bible and a good deal of Christian history and theology. He makes the point that God has a sense of humor—and we would hardly want to worship a god who did not take delight in wit, incongruity, surprise, and the sheer joy of life. Compact as it is, this is not a lightweight book. Give Darden a few minutes, and he just may change your view of preaching and worship, and put a new skip in your step."
—R. Alan Culpepper, Dean, McAfee School of Theology

Jesus Laughed

The Redemptive Power of Humor

Robert Darden

Abingdon Press
Nashville

JESUS LAUGHED: THE REDEMPTIVE POWER OF HUMOR

Copyright © 2008 by Abingdon Press

This book is printed on acid-free paper.

Library of Congress Cataloging-in-Publication Data

Darden, Bob, 1954-
   Jesus laughed : the redemptive power of humor / Robert Darden.
      p. cm.
   Includes bibliographical references.
   ISBN 978-0-687-64454-4 (binding:pbk., adhesive, perfect : alk. paper)
   1. Wit and humor—Religious aspects—Christianity. 2. Wit and humor in the Bible. I. Title.

BR115.H84D37 2008
233—dc22

                                                                 2008000449

All scripture quotations unless noted otherwise are taken from the New Revised Standard Version of the Bible, copyright 1989 by the Division of Christian Education of the National Council of the Churches of Christ in the United States of America. Used by permission. All rights reserved.

Scripture quotations marked (KJV) are from the King James or Authorized Version of the Bible.

Portions of this book, including the introduction, were inspired by or based on articles written by Robert Darden for Method-X (http://www.upperroom.org/methodx/default.asp); The High Calling: "Synchronized Swimming in the Pulpit" (http://thehighcalling.org/); and a talk I delivered at a deacon's retreat for Seventh & James Baptist Church, Waco, Texas.

09 10 11 12 13 14 15 16 17—10 9 8 7 6 5 4 3 2

MANUFACTURED IN THE UNITED STATES OF AMERICA

To my wife,
Dr. Mary Landon Darden,
who dances,
smiles
and laughs . . .

Just when I get my church all sorted out, sheep from the goats, saved from the damned, hopeless from the hopeful, somebody makes a move, gets out of focus, cuts loose, and I see why Jesus never wrote systematic theology. So you and I can give thanks that the focus of Christian thinking appears to be shifting from North America and northern Europe where people write rules and obey them, to places like Africa and Latin America where people still know how to dance.

—Will Willimon, *Leadership Journal,* Summer 1994.

Contents

Thanks to . . .

My parents: Robert and Jo Ann Darden (who laughed at my first jokes)

My kids: Dan Barkley, Mark and Rachel Menjivar, Van Darden

Seventh & James Baptist Church:
   The Rev. Raymond Bailey
   The congregation . . .
   and members of the Roundtable Sunday School Class:
            Sally Lynn Askins
            Jay Belew
            Mary Darden
            Ann McGlashan
            Mark W. Osler
            Ronald Stanke
            Lynn Tatum

Baylor University:
   Provost Randall O'Brien
   Dean of Arts & Sciences Lee Nordt
   Chair Clark Baker, Department of Journalism
   My friends and colleagues in the Journalism Department
   Sabbatical Committee (for a Summer 2007 sabbatical to complete the manuscript)
   University Research Committee (for a URC grant for 2007 to research and
            complete the manuscript)
   Professors in the Department of Religion and Truett Theological Seminary
            (who graciously provided me invaluable information
            whenever I needed it)

The staff at Moody Memorial Library, particularly the folks in Inter-Library Loan

My research assistants Kelly Owens and Elizabeth Suggs

My friends at Abingdon Press

My friends at the Trinity Foundation and *The Wittenburg Door*

Introduction

It has long been said that 11 a.m. on Sunday mornings is the most segregated hour of the week. I believe it. I also believe that it is the *dourest* hour of the week.

Christians, of all people, despite a *bazillion* wicked thoughts, secret obsessions, self-serving rationalizations and good-old-fashioned-no-matter-how-you-cut-it SIN in their lives ought to be LAUGHING OUT LOUD IN UNFETTERED HAPPINESS—**ESPECIALLY** ON SUNDAY—because they serve a Risen Savior who not only has redeemed them but guarantees them a place in heaven ANYWAY!

But we don't laugh.

Paul Tillich asks, "Is our lack of joy due to the fact that we are Christians, or to the fact we are not sufficiently Christian?" Then answers his own question a couple of sentences later:

> But let us be honest. Is there not enough foundation for criticism? Are not many Christians—ministers, students of theology, evangelists, missionaries, Christian educators and social workers, pious laymen and laywomen, even the children of such parents—surrounded by an air of heaviness, of oppressive sternness, of lack of humor and irony about themselves? We cannot deny this. Our critics outside the Church are right. And we ourselves should be even more critical than they, but critical on a deeper level. (Tillich 1955, 142–43)

In fact, there are people who claim that laughter, or humor of any kind, isn't Christian. There are folks who tell us that we shouldn't laugh because the Bible never says that Jesus laughed.

To that, I've got to . . . well . . . *laugh.*

If Jesus was fully human (as most Christians believe) as well as fully divine (as virtually all Christians believe), then Jesus laughed. Period. Finito. End of story. Human-types laugh. It's in our genetic hard wiring.

And God? God is *all over* laughter.

God's laughter, which began before the original creation, still rings throughout the universe today. It's not gravity that knits the universe, it's not Dark Matter . . . it's a Cosmic Chuckle. The Big Bang is just a pale reflection of the original Universal Guffaw. The Music of the Spheres? That's the sound of God's joy in creation. It's what binds the universe together.

Jesus Laughed: The Redemptive Power of Humor is a call to reclaim Holy Laughter for the church. This, I believe, can only be accomplished with a broad-based attack, one targeting every facet of the church and church life. *Jesus Laughed* will explore how and when the church lost this essential element, and then make the case that we need it back . . . badly . . . right this very minute.

This is not a Pollyanna approach. Bad things happen to reasonably good people. Terrible things. Yes, sometimes we do need to laugh to keep from crying. But sometimes we just need to . . . *cry*. Learning to adopt a joyful outlook, preserving the emotional energy necessary to confront disaster, and channeling anger and despair into useful energies are all facets of *Jesus Laughed*. I don't believe you can laugh your way to wellness, but a positive, laughter-infused, Christ-centered lifestyle can help you handle life's problems—in both sickness and in health.

The goal is to become more like the followers of St. Francis of Assisi, who were called *le Jongleur de Dieu*—"the tumblers of God" (Chesterton 2001, 78). They were compared to court jesters, circus performers, and street comics, so filled were they with the uncontainable joy of their salvation.

Not possible in this sophisticated day and age? Consider the words of a certain Mr. Nietzsche who says, in effect, "The redeemed ought to look more like it!" (*Blackfriars* 2004, vol. 85).

Or Evelyn Waugh, "I always think to myself: 'I know I am awful. But how much more awful I should be without the Faith'" (DeVille 2004, 73–74).

Imagine, indeed.

Jesus Laughed: The Redemptive Power of Humor won't harangue or shame you. This isn't a polemic. I don't know the "Seven Keys to a Laughter-Filled Life." I'm not going to convince anybody with lectures, plot points, or pithy sermons, and animated slide presentations scare me worse than clowns (brrr . . .).

Even if you agree with everything I say, you probably won't change overnight. If you're kind of grouchy, it took you a number of years to become a Grinch—it'll take a little while to turn you into Cindy Lou Who down in Whoville.

I do have two secret weapons on my side. First, *Jesus Laughed* features illustrations from Kevin Frank, a frequent contributor to the pages of *The Wittenburg Door*, the world's oldest, largest—and pretty much only—religious humor and satire magazine. *The Door* has been around more than thirty-five years. I've been the Senior Editor for the past twenty.

Second, I trained under the tutelage of *Door* founder Mike Yaconelli, who embodied the concept of the Holy Fool better than any person I've ever known. Mike was an open, honest, bumbling, courageous, surprising, fearless Christ-searcher. There was simply nothing he wouldn't do or say or wear or sing or dance if it would make even a tiny point about the "dangerous wonder" of a life spent in the love of Jesus Christ.

That meant, of course, that he was the *funniest* person I've ever known. Hands down.

My immediate goal is that this be a genuinely funny, helpful book that will give you some tools to alter your course a little . . . if necessary. And if you are already one of those rare people infused with genial good humor, the joy of Christ, and an expansive, loving spirit, maybe you'll buy it for your friends and help them out because you, my friend, are a rare and precious wonder.

In the end, my fondest desire with *Jesus Laughed* is to capture even the tiniest shard of this rare and wonderful insight by the German mystic Meister Eckhart:

Truly! Truly! By God! By God! Be as sure of it as you are that God lives: at the least good deed, the least bit of good will, the least of good desires, all the saints in heaven and on earth rejoice, and together with the angels, their joy is such that all the joy in this world cannot be compared to it. The more exalted a saint is, the greater his joy; but the joy of them all put together amounts to as little as a bean when compared to the joy of God over good deeds. For truly, God plays and laughs. (Blakney 1941, 143)

I believe with all my heart that God laughs and plays. I believe the loving God who created the universe wants us to be happy, to laugh, and to play.

As Mark Lowry says, "What healthy father *doesn't* love to hear his children laugh?" (2006, pers. comm.).

Worship a God who doesn't laugh? Preposterous!

CHAPTER 1

What Humor Is and How to Recognize It, Day or Night

To explain the nature of laughter and tears, is to account for the condition of human life; for it is in a manner compounded of these two! —William Hazlitt

Laughter. Humor. Gaiety. Mirth. Joy. Happiness.

If the thesis of this book is that these things really *do* matter to Christians and the church, then perhaps it's a good idea to explain/understand them and—in a perfect world—even learn how to use them. Your salvation does not depend on whether or not you get your pastor's latest joke. In fact, as we'll see, we're not even talking about jokes. But the quality of your life both before and after your salvation depends, in part, on your understanding of, as Hazlitt says, "the nature of laughter and tears" (1901, B). Or, as William H. Willimon expresses it: " . . . the very essence of grace is to receive the gift of laughter, especially when the joke is on us, particularly when the most laughable incongruities consist of the gap between who we are and who God would have us to be" (1986, 10).

Most of us have the tears bit figured out pretty well. We've already got two books in the Bible that spend 99 percent of their time telling us how crummy things are and how come we deserve it—Lamentations and Ecclesiastes. And you should probably avoid Job, James, and Revelation if you're a little blue too. For balance, you'd think there would be at least *one* book in the Bible titled "Delirious" or "Giddy with Delight" or even "Slap-Happy." But there's not.

Fortunately, humor and happiness are two intimately related concepts that you can learn to recognize, learn to reproduce, and even learn to internalize. And, in the pages ahead, I hope I'll be able to convince you that it is a *good* thing.

> [T]he ability to see the humor in things, or to create comic tales and rituals, is among the most profound and imaginative of human achievements. The comic sense is an important part of what it means to be human and humane. Without it we return to brutishness, and the Philistines are upon us. (Hyers 1981, 11)

From a scholarly, academic standpoint, science is still a little wobbly when it comes to explaining laughter and humor. Susanne Langer's pivotal *Feeling and Form* notes that laughter erupts, often unexpectedly, from a "surge of vital feeling." It's a complicated physiological and emotional process, she says, "a culmination of feeling— the crest of a wave of felt vitality." Langer further defines laughter as being more "elementary" than humor, since we can break into spontaneous laughter without any apparent stimulus or cause. "People laugh for joy in active sport, in dancing, in greeting friends; in returning a smile," she writes, "one acknowledges another person's worth instead of flaunting one's own superiority and finding him funny" (1953, 340, 341).

Comedy, still another separate quality, occurs when something is reinterpreted for us, somehow surprising us, creating something new:

> Humor, then, is not the essence of comedy, but only one of its most useful and natural elements. It is also its most problematical element, because it elicits from the spectators what appears to be a direct emotional response to persons on the stage, in no wise different from their response to actual people: amusement, laughter. (346)

Surprise

The most crucial concept related to humor that Langer identifies is *surprise*. Simply put, without surprise, there is no humor. Period.

Consider this: You're going to hear your favorite musical artist— Loreena McKennitt, Van Morrison, Prince, whoever—in concert. You scream madly each time he or she performs one of your favorite songs. And for an encore, you scream even louder to hear one (or more) of them again. If they comply, you leave feeling satisfied.

But say you've heard a very funny story. You want to share it with a friend. How do you preface your story? You say, "Stop me if you've heard this one before . . . "

Why? *Because if they've heard it before, there is no surprise.* Without the surprise, the story, the joke, isn't funny. The humor is in the surprise ending.

So the first great essential of humor/comedy is surprise.

Surprise comes from expectations being overturned. You expect one thing, but something unexpected happens. Surprise is—essentially—pulling the rug out from under someone's feet. But first you have to get them to stand on the rug . . .

In order to have surprise, you have to have the commonplace. The normal (or what appears to be normal) order of things; the everyday.

You'd expect the founders of our faith to be sterling individuals, saintly aesthetes who walk in God's favor. But the revered patriarchs and matriarchs of the Old Testament steal, lie, dissemble, flee in fear, kill, cavort with undesirables, fail repeatedly, and, in general, behave as badly as freshmen on Spring Break. If you're looking for heroes in the Bible, you're going to be surprised by the antics of Joseph, Isaac, David, Rachel, Tamar, Abigail, Jael, Solomon, Elijah, and all of the rest.

You'd expect the Founder of Christianity to speak in Grand Truths, in stirring, noble language, *not* to speak in riddles or tell little stories about goofy, common, infuriatingly normal people. And if you do fall for the Founder's gentle message, you're sure not expecting logic to be so consistently turned on its head—to conquer death, you only have to die; the last shall be first; it is better to be the servant than the master; you must be born *again;* and how come the rich man has such a long, hard slog if he's going to get to heaven?

You'd expect the long-awaited messiah to ride triumphantly into Jerusalem on a magnificent white stallion, at the head of a powerful army. But he trots in on a donkey, his way littered with palm fronds, surrounded by the common people of the city—some of whom may or may not call for his death in just a few days. Another surprise.

Oh, the Bible is *all over* surprise.

The best example of this is the surprise death and resurrection of Jesus Christ. The sheer, unadulterated, holy, outrageous unexpectedness of it is—sadly—lost to us today. We're told the story as soon as we're able to (barely) understand it. But two thousand years ago, the apostles were absolutely *gob-smacked* (to use one of my favorite British colloquialisms). Stunned. Flabbergasted. Mary didn't recognize Jesus in the garden—she thought he was the pool boy! John and Peter raced each other to the empty tomb and babbled about what they saw—or didn't see—so much so that the accounts in Matthew, Luke, and John are all slightly different.

The biggest joke of all, of course, is on Satan. That would be Easter, the day the bad guys thought they'd won—but didn't. The ancients have a long tradition of understanding Easter Sunday in terms of humor.

Early church fathers such as Augustine, Gregory of Nyssa, and even John of Chrysostom mused that God played a practical joke on the devil by raising Jesus from the grave. The Greek Orthodox Church even gave the joke the theological name of "risus paschalis"—Easter laughter (Segal 2001, 24).

In fact, Dante Alighieri called his greatest work, a cosmic exploration of the Christian experience, *The Comedy* (the "Divine" was added later—but as a title, it works even better; Musa 2003, xxx). Nobody was more surprised that glorious day two thousand years ago than Old Scratch.

Jürgen Moltmann (1972, 29–32) says that since historic times, Easter sermons in the Protestant tradition (which he notes wryly, is "well-known for its dryness") have often begun with a joke. In fact, he believes that 1 Corinthians 15:55-57 is really an Easter hymn that mocks and laughs at Satan:

> Death is swallowed up in victory.
> O death, where is thy victory?
> O death, where is thy sting?
> The sting of death is sin, and the power of sin is the law. But thanks be to God, who gives us victory through our Lord Jesus Christ.

The Greek Orthodox Church does it one better than the Protestants—many churches still follow the ancient custom of setting aside the entire day following Easter for twenty-four hours of non-stop humor, comedy, joking, and laughter because of:

> [T]he big joke God pulled on Satan in the Resurrection. Cosmos has been victorious over chaos, faith over doubt, trust over anxiety; and man is now truly free to laugh with the laughter of higher innocence. (Hyers 1969, 239)

Even C. S. Lewis got into the act. What's the first thing that Aslan does after the great lion is "resurrected" in *The Lion, the Witch and the Wardrobe*? He romps and plays with Lucy and Susan, "so that all three of them rolled over together in a **happy laughing** heap of fur and arms and legs" (Lewis 1978, 160; emphasis mine).

"The laughter of the universe is God's delight. It is the universal Easter laughter in heaven and on earth" (Moltmann and Moltmann-Wende 2003, 85). To create that kind of surprise—and thus humor—you have to take chances, be willing to alter the established order of things, dare to dream, and, most important, be willing to fail. Good comic writers daydream a lot, placing things in juxtaposition that have never been side by side before. That juxtaposition of two normal things sometimes creates an entirely new third thing.

One of the great masters of creating surprise was filmmaker Alfred Hitchcock. His best films are full of surprises. People went to see his movies *knowing* they were going to be surprised, and yet he still managed to surprise them repeatedly.

In any given Hitchcock film, a bad guy is usually waiting to jump out and kill Jimmy Stewart (it was almost always Jimmy Stewart) in a dark house. Everybody in the theater knows the bad guy is in the dark house except Jimmy Stewart. In fact, the bad guy's waiting down at the end of this long, dark hallway. Jimmy walks slowly down the hall, unconcerned, whistling a brave little tune. The anticipation builds. Just as he gets to the intersection with the next hallway where we're sure the bad guy waits . . . a flash of movement! Everybody shrieks! But it is only a cat. Jimmy relaxes. We relax and breathe a sigh of relief. Just a cat. It's then and only then that the bad guy jumps out! Double shriek!

Surprise!

A good surprise requires careful buildup—setting the stage, establishing the characters, creating expectations—then and only then, when the reader or congregation least expects it, pulling that rug out.

The result? People laugh. It's a natural, healthy response. A release.

One of the masters of using surprise to force both a sudden reevaluation of something that has become over-familiar and (sometimes) involuntary laughter is Flannery O'Connor. From her dark, disturbing story "The Violent Bear It Away" comes this snippet of the Christmas story, told by a child evangelist:

> She began again in a dirge-like tone. "Jesus came on cold straw, Jesus was warmed by the breath of an ox. 'Who is this?' the world said, 'who is this blue-cold child and this woman, plain as the winter? Is this the Word of God, this blue-cold child? Is this His will, this plain winter-woman?'
>
> "Listen you people!" she cried, "the world knew in its heart, the same you know in your hearts and I know in my heart. The world said, 'Love cuts like the cold wind and the will of God is plain as the winter. Where is the summer will of God? Where are the green seasons of God's will? Where is the spring and summer of God's will?'
>
> ". . . You know and I know," she said, turning again, "what the world hoped then. The world hoped old Herod would slay the right child, the world hoped old Herod wouldn't waste those children, but he wasted them. He didn't get the right one. Jesus grew up and raised the dead." (1964, 383)

There is a strange, chilling laugh that culminates in the final words of this paragraph. A wild, untamed quality. Humor, at its best, reorders the universe in new and exciting ways. What can you do but laugh at the wonder of it? It is in O'Connor's work that Frederick Buechner (a pretty funny guy himself) thinks he's found the wellspring of this kind of dangerous holy humor. He believes O'Connor is "one of the most *profoundly* funny writers" of the twentieth century:

I suppose it is precisely because she has a mystic's sense of what holiness truly is that she is able to depict in such a wry and sometimes uproarious way the freakish distortions that it suffers at the hands of a mad world. Her laughter comes from a very deep and holy place inside herself, in other words, and that is probably why it is so deeply infectious, why the comic element of her work is not merely one of its embellishments but of its very substance, as inseparable from the tragic element as grace is from sin. (Buechner 1992, 69)

Why is surprise the primary impetus of humor? It could be because it is at the root of "elemental laughter," the first giggles from a newborn child. Studies have shown that a baby's first laugh usually comes following the briefest of separations from the baby's mother and her sudden reappearance. It's that oldest of baby-games, "Peek-a-Boo." The most elemental laughter derives from the reunion of family. And isn't that what the Easter Surprise, the Easter Laughter is all about? But first you must have the surprise (Segal 2001, 25).

In the end, without surprise life has a numbing sameness. Once we excise the possibility of amazement from our lives, existence veers dangerously close to tedium. It's that lack of predictability that makes a long prison sentence so soul-sapping. Life shouldn't be like a prison sentence.

Commonality and Community

The second element necessary to create quality humor is the establishment of a shared community. The best humor is about the people (or people types and—as a last resort—stereotypes) you know. You're at a party. Suddenly, a guy gets a banana cream pie in the face. That's mildly amusing. But if the guy getting the pie in the kisser is your obnoxious brother-in-law, now *that's* funny!

That's why the best comedians quickly create a community of easily recognizable characters, people you can identify with. That's why they pick on popular (or unpopular) politicians, entertainers, and athletes. You know them; you know something about them. No matter how funny he is, a British comic making wildly clever observations about English politicians probably isn't going to get many laughs in Omaha or Waco. We just don't know those guys. The connection isn't there. It isn't funny.

That means the best humor is narrative-based, not joke-based. Jokes and puns are the *lowest* kind of humor, a smile-inducing (at best), momentary break from the norm. But if you're writing or talking about real people, in real settings, facing real issues and problems, then you've created community and the potential for real humor. The humor flows out of the characters naturally. The reader/viewer/congregation invests in these characters and empathizes with them—even if they're animated, like Bugs Bunny, Nemo, Shrek, or the gang in Peanuts or Bloom County.

Related to this, humor is always funnier in a group, just as faith is better and stronger in a group. Watching a comic DVD alone on your home computer may be only mildly amusing. But watch it with a group of good friends and it is riotous. You may indeed be able to worship God in your own way out in the fields and by the beach. But it is better as part of a loving, wounded, searching community.

To create true, enduring humor, you must create community—think of old family friends sitting around talking . . . the laughter rolls naturally, regularly, and often. They're not *doing* anything but talking, and they're having a great time. As a kid listening in to these conversations, I didn't get it. How come they were having so much fun? All they were doing was talking.

A humorist's greatest challenge is creating community and a tacitly acknowledged group of shared assumptions in a room of disparate strangers. That's why pastors have it easier. They have a common language, a common set of known, recognizable characters, and they have a community.

That's why the best stories, the funniest stories from the pulpit or in print are—whenever possible—real stories about real people. There is a significant difference in listener investment between a story that begins:

"A guy walks into a church and says . . . "

And the same story that begins:

"Pat Robertson walks into First Baptist Dallas and says . . . "

Of course, we can laugh to ourselves. And no, we don't need other people around to be funny or to find something funny. But humor is a natural part of a shared community, it infuses the whole, makes it brighter, warmer, deeper, better. It's better to be around other caring people when you're down. And let's face it, not every day is full of sunshine and daffodils. Somebody has been through it—whatever "it" is—before. Both large and small crises are better shared.

If you're creating community, then shared anxiety is anxiety diffused.

That's what makes a comic like Paula Poundstone or Ellen Degeneres (or the late Grady Nutt) so special. They take our anxieties and translate them into everyday life—into the things we automatically, unconsciously think and do—and expose them to a wider audience. While you're laughing at one of their routines, you're thinking, "Hey, I've done that" or "Hey, I've said that."

Always Aim Up

We love to see the pompous, the self-important, and the powerful tweaked. This, by the way, is also us. We appear pompous, self-important, and powerful to somebody else. That means the third quality of humor is that the best humor is directed at us or somebody higher up the food chain. That's why national politicians, movie stars, and famous athletes are such fertile fodder for humor.

If humor is sometimes a reaction to tragedy—we're laughing in relief that someone else got the pie in the face and not us—then it really works best when it involves somebody bigger, stronger, faster, smarter, or wealthier. The same things you'd tease Donald Trump or Tom Cruise about, you'd never think of teasing someone poor or powerless about. That's bullying, and it is never funny.

It makes sense, then, that the best humor is usually by the *outs* about the *ins*. That's why the Jews have a legendary propensity for humor, whether it is self-deprecating (think of Tevya from *Fiddler on the Roof*) or observations about a mad, incredibly powerful universe that's threatening to destroy them (think Woody Allen). That's why there are so many brilliant African American comics, from Richard Pryor through Eddie Murphy and Chris Rock. The underdogs have survived (in part) by poking fun at the *overdogs*. It's saying, "You may have the power, but you can't control how we think."

That's why you don't see rich, handsome, debonair heroes in romantic comedies very often. Those are the guys the humor is directed against. Instead, the best *rom-coms* (as they're called in the industry) now feature everyman actors like Ben Stiller, John Cusack, or Jack Black. Think Napoleon Dynamite or a young Tom Hanks.

Here Beginneth the Digression

One major variant form of comedy is romantic comedy, actually a whole separate genre unto itself. It has been one of the most enduring staples of entertainment since the time of the Greeks and Romans. Shakespeare and Moliere are justly celebrated for their romantic comedies. And, with the rise of movies, some of the most successful films of all time have been released under this general heading—*It Happened One Night, Some Like It Hot, Annie Hall, Tootsie, A Fish Called Wanda*, and *Sleepless in Seattle*.

The best rom-coms follow a certain "formula"—two appealing characters (generally a boy and girl, although the times they are a'changing). They meet "cute." They generally don't like each other at first—they apparently have nothing in common but their mutual dislike. Each must have something that the other needs to be a complete person. In *A Fish Called Wanda*, Archie (John Cleese) is uptight, rigid, and beaten down—he needs to be more spontaneous and alive. But he is loyal to a fault. Wanda (Jamie Lee Curtis) is sneaky, thieving, and deceitful—but she is nothing if not spontaneous and alive. Each needs something the other has. Only when they learn from one another, and can internalize those traits and become "whole" will they eventually get together.

According to a charming article by Nehama Aschkenasy, there is at least one romantic comedy in the Bible, the story of Ruth. This little book has all of the characteristics of a comedy: a plucky heroine who goes from distress to success, a reversal of fortune, the women of Bethlehem serving as a (sometimes snarky) Greek chorus, suspense, epiphany, and a happy ending all around.

But Aschkenasy creates a convincing argument that this is a classic rom-com as well. In addition to everything listed above, we find two distinct, opposite characters (a shy older man who is somewhat pompous and lonely and a brave, impetuous, unconventional younger woman), comic wordplay, and a "war" between the sexes.

At its best, comedy has always been serious business, pointing out the absurdities of the human condition, highlighting human frailty and folly, while at the same time delighting us with redemption of a happy ending. (Aschkenasy 2006, 31–44)

Here Endeth the Digression

This concept plays out beautifully in the Bible. The worst, most embarrassing stories are told about the kings and patriarchs. It's not hard to imagine generations of Hebrew children sitting around the campfire, snickering at the loony adventures of some of these people. They're constantly being tricked and befuddled. They lust after forbidden women and forbidden gods, they betray and are betrayed, they say and do the dumbest things at the worst times. Noah bends the elbow too many times. Jonah whines and sulks. Moses whines and sulks. Elijah whines and sulks.

By the way, one of the great funny images in the Bible is in 1 Kings in this scene between Elijah and Ahab at the end of the great drought:

> Then he said, "Go say to Ahab, 'Harness your chariot and go down before the rain stops you.'" In a little while the heavens grew black with clouds and wind; there was a heavy rain. Ahab rode off and went to Jezreel. **But the hand of the LORD was on Elijah; he girded up his loins and ran in front of Ahab to the entrance of Jezreel**.
> (1 Kings 18:44-46, emphasis mine)

A white-haired prophet hiking up his skirt and outrunning a chariot all the way home? What the heck was *that* all about?!

The New Testament (N.T.) is likewise full of holier-than-thou folks getting punctured. Jesus' most biting satire and severe tongue-lashings are reserved not for the humble farmers and merchants but for the cultural elite—scribes, lawyers, Sadducees, Pharisees, and priests. At one point, he makes a dangerous jibe about the despotic ruler of the day, calling King Herod "that fox" (Luke 13:32). Observing and commenting on the smug, the oppressors, and the powerful was apparently a national pastime in those days, and the Romans and the Jewish elite made a great, shared target for humor. Jesus was hounded by these people and we, alas, only have a few of the doubtless thousands of funny barbs he made in his exchanges with them. They were probably a source of endless amusement among his followers, who recounted them for days on the dusty roads from Dan to Beersheba.

And so a great source of humor comes from observing and commenting on the powerful, the smug, the oppressors, and the rich. In the end, the key here, of course, is to remember that to most of the world, *we are* the rich, the powerful, the holier-than-thou types. So it's probably best—if you want to be genuinely funny—to aim the bulk of your barbs at yourself or above.

Artful Elaboration

A less charitable person might call this category "Exaggeration." As we'll see, there is a fine line between the two, especially when it comes to storytelling and humor. But for now, we'll use the terms interchangeably.

If the ancient equation of *Tragedy + Time = Comedy* is correct, then is it right to ask, "Is this really exaggeration?" After all, our memory plays tricks on us. The fish that got away gets bigger with each retelling. The near miss on the highway gets more hair-raising each time it is told. The pranks of our college days grow in stature with each reunion. We instinctively understand and come to expect this; it is part and parcel of the storytelling tradition. For comic effect, the good storyteller takes the basic facts, emphasizes certain ones and downplays or omits others. Part of the fun is acknowledging the skill a storyteller applies to those little touches. In *Annie Hall* (1977), Annie (Diane Keaton) sends Alvy Singer (Woody Allen) to kill a spider in the bathroom. Armed with a tennis racket, he marches reluctantly into battle, only to pop out a heartbeat later. "Honey, there's a spider in your bathroom the size of a Buick!!"

Comedy observes the human condition and comments on it, some-times using artful elaboration to bring some facet of our lives or beliefs into high contrast or relief.

A really clever, totally and unexpectedly outlandish exaggeration is funny in and of itself. This can be done in a number of ways, including incongruity. (If coconut oil comes from coconuts and olive oil comes from olives, where does baby oil come from?)

One of the great places to find humorous exaggeration is—sur-prise!—in the book of Proverbs. As kids we used to get a kick out of reading these couplets, generally when we should have been listening to the sermon in church. You've got to wonder if the writer of Proverbs was referring to someone in particular in chapter 26:

> Like an archer who wounds everybody
>   is one who hires a passing fool or drunkard.
> Like a dog that returns to its vomit
>   is a fool who reverts to his folly.
> Do you see persons wise in their own eyes?
>   There is more hope for fools than for them.
> The lazy person says, "There is a lion in the road!
>   There is a lion in the streets!"

> As a door turns on its hinges,
>   so does a lazy person in bed.
> The lazy person buries a hand in the dish,
>   and is too tired to bring it back to the mouth. (Proverbs 26:10-16)

This reads like a scene out of *The Big Lebowski*—and what's with the lion thing? Is that why the lazy dude stays home that day?

Jesus knew how to turn a phrase, too. In his teaching on hypocrisy in Matthew 7:1-5, Jesus could have said, "Don't be hypocrites, y'all!" Instead, he memorably uses artful elaboration for vivid comic effect:

> "Why do you see the speck in your neighbor's eye . . . ? Or how can you say to your neighbor, 'Let me take the speck out of your eye,' while the log is in your own eye?" (Matthew 7:3-4)

He could have just told the Rich Young Ruler in Matthew 19:23-24, "Sorry, pal, unless you give up your beloved possessions for something of eternal value, you're not going to heaven." Instead, he uses a shocking exaggeration that still has the power to surprise today:

> Then Jesus said to his disciples, "Truly I tell you, it will be hard for a rich person to enter the kingdom of heaven. Again, I tell you, it is easier for a camel to go through the eye of a needle than for someone who is rich to enter the kingdom of God."

In both cases, there were probably shocked gasps and titters of laughter in the crowd. Likewise, no one really thought the Pharisees were actually "whitewashed tombs" in Matthew 23:27—but the dramatic use of exaggeration created a timeless image.

At the other end of the spectrum, Jesus calls the brothers John and James *Boanerges,* that is, "Sons of Thunder" in Mark 3:17, although we don't ever hear much about James—no doubt he was the shy, retiring, mousy type. And did Jesus nickname Simon "Peter" *(petra—rock)* in Matthew 16:18 because he was solid or because he was a little dense at times? Artful elaboration is one of the linchpins of satire and sarcasm.

Other Laughter

The human animal can find humor in the craziest places.

The Dark Side

There is, for example, the humor that sustains people through the darkest, bitterest times. One of the more surprising places to find humor is in *The Diary of Anne Frank*, the journal of the brave little girl who chronicled daily life in occupied Holland, where each noise could lead to discovery and gruesome death for the small group. She writes freely of the laughter that still resounds in their cramped attic prison, including this heartbreaking exchange with her shy, almost-boyfriend Peter on March 23, 1944:

> Peter so often used to say, "Do laugh, Anne!" This struck me as odd, and I asked, "Why must I always laugh?"
>
> "Because I like it; you get such dimples in your cheeks when you laugh; how do they come, actually?"
>
> "I was born with them. I've got one in my chin, too. That's my only beauty!"
>
> "Of course not, that's not true."
>
> "Yes, it is, I know quite well that I'm not a beauty; I never have been and never shall be."
>
> "I don't agree at all, I think you're pretty."
>
> "That's not true."
>
> "If I say so, then you can take it from me it is!"
>
> Then I naturally said the same of him.

I hear a lot from all sides about the sudden friendship. We don't take much notice of all of this parental chatter, their remarks are so feeble. Have the two sets of parents forgotten their own youth? It seems like it, at least they seem to take us seriously, if we make a joke, and laugh at us when we are serious. (Frank 1959, 175–76)

Within weeks of writing these words, this brave, joyful little girl will die in a Nazi concentration camp.

This is related to the grim humor that sometimes emerges when people are in great danger, such as war. There are entire books that provide examples of this "gallows" humor (which is not all that different from foxhole conversions and the saying that there are no atheists in foxholes). One representative example comes from the bloody battles of the Normandy invasion in World War II. A German platoon hidden in a church wreaks havoc with advancing English soldiers until, after great cost, the church is taken. Immediately afterward, a British NCO makes a hasty report to his superior:

"Was the church badly damaged?" asked the colonel.
"Not inside it wasn't, sir . . . We just knocked the top off; we wouldn't have touched it if the snipers hadn't been there. And when I went in, sir, I did take my hat off." (Hastings 1985, 456)

Here Beginneth the Digression

Few stories are more stirring—and defiantly funny—than this one from the Battle of the Bulge during World War II, the great German winter offensive of December 1944 in the Ardennes Forest. A massive Nazi combined army group overwhelms all before it, only to be stalled by remnants of various U.S. Army divisions. The situation appears to be hopeless and the German commander demands that the town of Bastogne surrender or face annihilation. Brigadier-General Anthony C. McAuliffe's formal written response read as follows:

To the German Commander:
    "Nuts!"
—The American Commander

Naturally, the German parlementaires were confused by the general's curt response, but were assured that the answer was not in the affirmative. McAuliffe's men held and the tide was turned. (Hastings, 464–66)

Here Endeth the Digression

In fact, there are those who believe that this kind of dark humor actually borders on the holy. When it happens—laughter in the face of the greatest odds and darkest moments—Reinhold Niebuhr says it is proof that the human animal understands its place in the cosmic scheme of things. It is a sign that for all our pride, we understand at the most basic level Who is in charge:

> To meet the disappointments and frustrations of life, the irrationalities and contingencies with laughter, is a high form of wisdom. Such laughter does not obscure or defy the dark irrationality. It merely yields to it without too much emotion and friction. A humorous acceptance of fate is really the expression of a high form of self-detachment. (Niebuhr 1946, 126)

The Laughter of Innocence

Still another kind of humor is the spontaneous laughter that comes from watching children innocently explore their new world, puppies tripping over their ears, and old friends reuniting after long separations.

Unfortunately, there aren't many of these small, intimate scenes in the Bible, although I feel certain they happened hundreds, perhaps thousands, of times daily then, just as they do now.

D'oh!

One last variation on the theme—the humor we all experience when we watch someone who is clearly at fault desperately dissembling and rationalizing. It's the old, "I can't believe he's just said that" kind of humor. There's probably not much that is redemptive in this kind of laughter—but hey, we're human after all. My favorite example of this funny/sad humor is the side-splitting BBC comedy series, *Fawlty Towers*, where Basil (John Cleese)—a man of endless pretensions and vanity—tries to run a small hotel in England's West Country. Each episode ends with Basil's schemes and dreams in tatters and Basil humiliated once again.

The Bible has a couple of such moments, but none to compare with the life of Aaron, the brother of Moses and the most Teflon-coated character in the entire O.T. Among his best bits is Exodus 32. Moses tarries a bit too long up on the mountain with Yahweh and the Ten Commandments. The Hebrew people get antsy, want a god, and Aaron happily obliges. Yahweh, of course, gets wind of this idol-making, and Moses just barely saves the Israelites from total annihilation. Moses storms down the mountain, shatters the tablets, hammers the golden calf into little pieces, dumps the pieces into the Kool-Aid, and makes the people drink it. Then he grabs Aaron and shouts, "What is the meaning of this?!" Startled, Aaron drops his Sudoku and stammers:

> "Do not let the anger of my lord burn hot; you know the people, that they are bent on evil. They said to me, 'Make us gods, who shall go before us; as for this Moses, the man who brought us up out of the land of Egypt, we do not know what has become of him.' So I said to them, 'Whoever has gold, take it off'; so they gave it to me, and I threw it into the fire, and out came this calf!" (Exodus 32:22-25)

In other words, the people MADE him do it—because you know how wicked they are—then we threw the gold in the fire and—wouldn't you know it—this Golden Calf JUST APPEARS! Who would have thought it?

You have to shake your head and laugh at Aaron's *chutzpah,* but once again he wiggles out of a tight spot unscathed during the killings that follow. At the end of another abortive coup against Moses, it is Miriam who is struck with leprosy; not Aaron, who once again weasels his way out of punishment in Numbers 12:10.

Why is this funny? In part, because we see ourselves in Aaron. We try this sort of thing all of the time—with God, with our boss, with our spouse—desperately rationalizing, inventing, interpreting even as the flop sweat forms on our upper lip. I'm Aaron. And thus, as John Morreall (1999) notes:

> Humor is especially useful in getting people to see themselves and everything in their lives with emotional disengagement, from a higher, more objective perspective. They can poke fun at themselves, and at the traditions and authorities they follow. They think flexibly and critically, even iconoclastically, as Jesus did. (123)

Especially in the Bible

If that's true—and I believe it is—then we should be open to the fact that humor and laughter and comedy are everywhere, all around us, even in the Bible, *especially* in the Bible. The basic elements necessary to create something funny are all there: surprise, commonality and community, always aiming up, and artful elaboration. So why don't more people think of the Bible when the word *humor* comes up?

"One reason for our failure to laugh is our extreme familiarity with the received text," writes Elton Trueblood, who knows of what he speaks. "The words seem to us like old coins, in which the edges have been worn smooth and the engravings have become almost indistinguishable" (1964, 18).

Anybody can write and speak with humor. However, I don't know of anybody who is *naturally* funny (although the late Mike Yaconelli and Tony Campolo come close). It takes work. It takes practice. It's a muscle that needs to be exercised daily. If you think Leno or Letterman are funny, watch the closing credits—it takes dozens of writers, full-time and freelance, to create their shows, including the opening monologues (which are, let's be honest, pretty hit and miss these days).

But when a writer does combine all of the above while weaving a story *and* striving to say Something That Matters, that's worth celebrating. I could close this chapter with any number of examples that do exactly that. But I've chosen to end with a couple of segments from Anne Lamott's *Plan B: Further Thoughts on Faith* (2005) because she's so wonderfully transparent (especially for a Christian), and because she does approach everything with a childlike innocence, and because I *know* there is laughter in the church she describes. In this scene, she's been asked to establish a Sunday school in an old senior center:

> Our building was falling to pieces. I like this in a church. You see more clearly how held together we are, in spite of the sags and creakiness and the buckled floors . . .
>
> One day at the senior center, I could feel something tugging on my inside sleeve, which is the only place I ever hear from God: on the shirtsleeve of my heart. I understood that someone needed to start a school, because it was the right thing to do, and most important, I needed to make church more fun for Sam [her son].

> I know that with writing, you start where you are, and you flail around for a while, and if you keep doing it, every day you get closer to something good. Carolyn Myss said that we are responsible not for the outcome of things, but only for the ingredients, so Kris and I

bought everything we could think of that young children would need to learn about God: juice boxes, blankets, beach balls, moist towelettes, a children's Bible, a boom box, and art supplies.

"And what will we teach them?" Keris asked. This was a problem. I don't know much about God; only that He or She is love, and is not American, or male. I do love Jesus, and I'm nuts about his mother. Mary Oliver said something to the effect that the best sermon she ever heard was the sun. I thought, that's the sort of thing we'll teach. (60–61)

CHAPTER 2

For the Bible Tells Me So

Man does not bring on his own unhappiness, and suffering is really God's will, although why He gets such a kick out of it is beyond me. Certain Orthodox tribes believe suffering is the only way to redeem oneself, and scholars write of a cult called the Essenes, who deliberately went around bumping into walls. God, according to the later books of Moses, is benevolent, although there are still a great many subjects He'd rather not go into. —Woody Allen (1971)

So, just what *does* the Bible say about the presence or absence of laughter, of humor, of joy, of happiness in life? Um, quite a lot actually. The place to turn to is, I kid you not, *The Strongest Strong's Exhaustive Concordance of the Bible* (Strong, Kohlenberger, and Swanson 2001, 499, 667, 779), which is roughly the size of a full-grown Alsatian. It supersedes its less successful predecessor, *The Relatively Robust Strong's Exhaustive Concordance of the Bible. Strong's Strongest* lists:

15 uses of the word *mirth*
18 uses of the word *laugh*
13 uses of the word *laughed*
 7 uses of the word *laughter*
 1 use of the word *laugheth*
 1 use of the word *laughing*
28 uses of the word *happy*

The most famous sequence in the Bible involving laughter is also the first, the Genesis 17–18 account of the birth of Isaac. This sequence follows the decidedly *un*funny stories of Ishmael and Sarai. Despite Abram's unbelief, the Lord brags on the ninety-nine-year-old and tells him that he'll be the father of nations and that he'll have millions upon millions of descendants, that he'll be renamed "Abraham," *and* that he'll have the honor of experiencing the very first circumcision.

Abram, now Abraham, is understandably underwhelmed, especially the circumcision bit, and probably secretly wonders if a nice tattoo wouldn't do just as well.

But the Lord isn't finished yet. Next, the Lord renames Sarai as "Sarah" and says that she'll be the mother of those millions of descendants.

Abraham's response? He laughs. He literally rolls on the ground laughing. "Me? A dad? Old Sarah, a mom? That's rich," he thinks. But Abraham didn't get to the century mark by laughing at the Creator of the Known Universe. At least not out loud.

So at last, Abraham catches his breath. "*Heh heh heh,* good one, Lord. You really had me going there. I'll bet everyone up in heaven is going, 'Gotcha!'" Abraham wipes the tears from his eyes. "Still, it's great that Ishmael will do well. He's a good boy."

Nonplussed, the Lord tells Abraham to start stocking up on ice cream and pickles, because Sarah is going to be in the family way very, very soon (see Genesis 17:1-27).

The second description of this particular encounter appears in Genesis 18 (the so-called Yahwist version). This time, when the dialogue is repeated, Sarah is hiding behind the tent flap and listening. When the Lord gets to the bit about Sarah having kids, she busts out giggling hysterically.

> "After I have grown old, and my husband is old, shall I have pleasure?" The LORD said to Abraham, "Why did Sarah laugh, and say, 'Shall I indeed bear a child, now that I am old?' Is anything too wonderful for the LORD? At the set time I will return to you, in due season, and Sarah shall have a son." But Sarah denied, saying, "I did not laugh"; for she was afraid. He said, "Oh yes, you did laugh." (Genesis 18:12-15)

Is this an example of gentle, whimsical, self-deprecating laughter, an old woman remembering the good old days when she and her husband were sexually active? Or is it bitter laughter, a knee-jerk reaction to a suggestion about something that—at their age—is now a physical impossibility? Is she giggling or scoffing? There are, after all, many kinds of laughter. Or is Sarah just worried about how foolish she'll look suddenly pregnant (Gilhus 1997, 24–25)?

Likewise, is Abraham's laughter at the news mocking disbelief or an involuntary response of joy and astonishment?

And how come the Lord gets ticked off at Sarah and not Abraham? Apparently, whatever kind of laughing Abraham did was okay, while Sarah's little outburst wasn't. But Frederick Buechner insists that Sarah's response is both "high and holy laughter" (1979, author's note).

Either way, this is the first instance in the Bible where laughter gets the *laugher* in trouble.

The Bible interrupts the story here to insert some uncommonly unpleasant business about a couple of cities named Sodom and Gomorrah (if you're not familiar with this story, avoid this bit if you have delicate sensibilities) and King Abimelech leching after the one-hundred-year-old Sarah (actually, this bit may upset you more).

In Genesis 21, when the blessed event arrives, Sarah names the baby Isaac, which means "He laughs." This is apparently acceptable because the implication is not of the derisive laughter that springs from disbelief.

So here, in microcosm, is the root of our first problem: what kind of laughter are we talking about—sardonic, rueful laughter or the unfettered laughter of a happy, joyous heart? For a clear example of the latter kind, we'll have to keep exegetin' our way through the text . . .

Isaac has various adventures until we get to the cycle of stories about his own son, Jacob, and Jacob's wives Rachel and Leah in Genesis 29–31. One of Jacob's children (with Leah's maidservant Zilpah) is a boy, whom Leah names Asher, meaning "Happy" or "Happy am I!" (Genesis 30:12).

But perhaps the first recorded moment of *genuine* humor occurs in Genesis 31. Jacob is now on the outs with Laban, the father of Rachel and Leah. Laban, remember, was the one who tricked that Trickster Jacob into marrying both of his daughters. Jacob has been living in very close proximity to Laban and feeling increasingly squeezed by his father-in-law. One night he orders his retinue to sneak out into the darkness. Rachel (perhaps feeling that she and Jacob didn't get a fair shake in the birthright business) creeps into Laban's tent and steals his household gods.

After a few days, Laban realizes both Jacob *and* his household gods are gone and immediately sets out in pursuit with a formidable force. He eventually catches Jacob and berates him publicly, then demands the return of his little gods. But Rachel covertly places them in her saddle and sits on them . . . household gods, by the way, were probably not the softest padding available, even in 2000 B.C.

Laban's men ransack Jacob's tents—nothing. Jacob (who doesn't know about Rachel's little bit of pillage) pompously swears that whoever has stolen his father-in-law's gods will be killed. Rachel smiles blandly and squirms slightly in her seat. Finally, Laban's men search the caravan riders and their belongings. When they get to Rachel, she gives her father her most dazzling smile and says, "Hi daddy. Sorry I can't give you a big hug, but I'm having my monthly visit from Alice—well, you know how it is . . ."

Laban most certainly does *not* know how it is, but if there were ritual rites of purity back in that paternalistic society, coming in contact with a woman during her period was a big no-no. He smiles and nervously declines.

In the end, nobody finds nothin'. Laban and Jacob kiss and make up, and Rachel and Leah, for whatever reason, get clean away with daddy's household deities (see Genesis 31:14-42).

In the hands of the right director, this would be a very funny bit of cinema business. The daughters—who had been bought and sold like cattle—have the last laugh on their old man while oblivious Jacob looks on helplessly. You know the girls had a good laugh at Laban's expense that night, and probably didn't tell Jacob about their little bit of pilferage until they were many, many miles away.

There is another funny little story in a most unexpected place, Numbers 22. The Israelites are up to their old idol-worshiping ways, so the Lord uses Balaam, a foreign prophet, to set them straight. Balaam is actually on a mission to denounce the Lord for King Balak, but God appears to him in a dream and convinces him to switch sides. The next morning, Balaam saddles up his donkey and heads to Moab, even though the Lord has told him to wait. This is what is known as "foreshadowing," boys and girls.

They're trotting along nicely when, suddenly, Balaam's ass (alas, we never learn his name) sees an angel with a nasty-looking sword blocking the path. Balaam can't—or won't—see it. The donkey wisely turns aside. Three times Balaam urges the donkey forward, striking him each time he refuses.

Finally, the donkey has had enough. He turns to Balaam and chews him out for all of the unnecessary smiting, then informs his rider that an angel is barring the way. Balaam, at last, sees the angel and repents of the ass-smiting. Balaam will go on to deliver four powerful messages (or oracles) to Israel.

It's one of only two instances in the Bible where an animal speaks (the other being the serpent in the garden of Eden), and the tale of Balaam's smart-mouth donkey has been popular in Jewish households for a couple of millennia. (I've imagined the ass has a voice like the Eddie Murphy donkey in *Shrek*.)

Here Beginneth the Digression

There is a good—if ancient—Quaker talking-donkey joke too. A Quaker is trying to harness his lone mule to plow a rocky field. The donkey bites him. The Quaker tries again. The donkey kicks him in the stomach. Finally, the man gets the animal hooked to the plow, and the donkey turns and runs the plow over the Quaker's foot.

Pushed beyond human endurance, the gentle Quaker limps around to the donkey's face, holds him nose to nose, and says, "Thou knowest I shall not strike thee, friend ass. Thou knowest I shall not curse thee, either. But what thou doesn't knowest is that I can sell thee to the Southern Baptist down the road."

Here Endeth the Digression

Job, Laugh Riot of the OT

For the next use of the actual word *laugh*, we have to forge ahead to that laugh-riot, the book of Job. In fact, J. William Whedbee (1977, 1) argues that the entire book is a comedy! There are perhaps seven references to our word here, each with a slightly different spin (emphasis throughout is mine).

1. Job 5:22

His "friend" Eliphaz corrects some of Job's "errors," saying that whoever the Lord chastises, the Lord also rewards:
"At destruction and famine, you shall **laugh**,
    and shall not fear the wild animals of the earth."

2. Job 8:21

His "friend" Bildad urges Job to repent, saying that he'll be happier if he does so:
"He will yet fill your mouth with **laughter**,
    and your lips with shouts of joy."

3. Job 9:23

Job responds to his friends and asks who his mediator will be during his time of trial:
"When disaster brings sudden death,
    he mocks [other translations use '**laughs**'] at the calamity
        of the innocent."

4. Job 12:4

Job tells his friends it's easy for them to give free advice, *he's* the one who has been humiliated and hurt:
"I am a **laughingstock** to my friends;
    I, who called upon God and he answered me,
    a just and blameless man, I am a **laughingstock**."

5. Job 22:19-20

The latecomer Eliphaz, who is just a little full of himself, opines that the wicked may think they don't need God, but they'll soon find out otherwise:
"The righteous see it and are glad;
    the innocent **laugh** them to scorn,

saying, 'Surely our adversaries are cut off,
    and what they left, the fire has consumed.'"

6. Job 29:24

Here Job finishes his defense; reiterating that he was (and is) innocent and that he'll be back on top someday. This is the King James Version of Job's retelling about his glory days:

"If I **laughed** on them, they believed it not; and the light of my countenance they cast not down."

7. Job 41:29

Finally, God answers everybody, shaming them for their doubt, asking who else could have made the wonders of the universe, including Leviathan, which may be a giant crocodile or nigh-invulnerable dragon:

"Clubs are counted as chaff;
    it **laughs** at the rattle of javelins."

In all but #2 and perhaps #6 (the language here is so obscure, so archaic, most reference books disagree on what's actually being said), this is a scoffing, sneering laughter—the kind of laughter that's tinged with superiority. If that were the *only* kind of laughter mentioned in the O.T., it would make sense that later interpreters would be dead-set against it.

But the laughter in #2 is the kind of laughter that comes from living a contented, blessed life, a spontaneous, joyous laughter that cannot be contained. That's the good stuff. How can anybody be against that kind of laughter?

As we'll soon see, quite a few people were . . . but now back to *scorn*.

More Scorn

The other kind, the scornful laughter, dominates the humor references in the rest of the O.T. It takes several forms, but the underlying meaning is almost always the same.

Scornful laughter by enemies at the long-suffering writer or prophet:

Psalm 22:7	Proverbs 1:26
Psalm 52:6	2 Chronicles 30:10
Psalm 80:6	Nehemiah 2:19

Scornful laughter by the Lord at the feeble plans of men and women:

Psalms 2:4	Isaiah 37:22 (a repeat of 2 Kings 19:21)
Psalms 37:13	Most of Isaiah 44
Psalms 59:8	Ezekiel 23:32
2 Kings 19:21	

The writer laughing scornfully at his/her enemies, who are eventually going to be utterly destroyed by God anyway:

Psalm 52:6 (the psalmist counts himself among the righteous here)

"Wisdom" laughing at the feeble plans of men and women:

Proverbs 1:26

The most famous of the Preacher's mournful observations on laughter and mirth:

Sorrow is better than **laughter**,
for by sadness of countenance, the heart is made glad.
The heart of the wise is in the house of mourning;
but the heart of fools is in the house of **mirth**.
It is better to hear the rebuke of the wise
than to hear the song of fools.
For like the crackling of thorns under a pot,
so is the **laughter** of fools;
this is also vanity. (Ecclesiastes 7: 3-6)

. . . lots of scornful laughter here. And if that's why everybody is so down on laughter and humor, then I can dig it.

Fortunately, there are some *other* things going on in the OT

One of the most elegant and melancholy of all the Psalms is the wistful Psalm 126. I particularly like the King James translation of verses one through three:

When the Lord turned again the captivity of Zion, we were like them that dream.

Then was our mouth filled with laughter, and our tongue with singing: then said they among the heathen, The Lord hath done great things for them.

The Lord hath done great things for us; whereof we are glad.

Here laughter is a good thing, a natural outpouring of happiness by a people who were content in their own land, who once enjoyed the protection and affection of their God. A thousand miles away, now in exile, the psalmist paints a picture of their lost home in detail—and everywhere there is spontaneous laughter and joy. At least, that's how the psalmist remembers it. Patrick Laude cites the laughter in this verse as "a kind of inebriation with God's presence and immanent mercy. It is as if God's intrinsic laughter, as overflowing joy, were communicated to those whom He protects and loves" (2005, 133).

Ah, Elijah

There are other kinds of laughter in the O.T. One good example is found in the story of Elijah, which has some marvelously funny characters and bits. It reads like a sitcom from Jewish television, circa 1500 B.C.

1 Kings 17–18
Elijah appears suddenly as a prophetic thorn in the side of King Ahab and his Canaanite wife Jezebel, during a particularly dark time in the history of Israel. Only a few people still believe in the Lord, the land is gripped by a ferocious drought, and Baal worship is the order of the day. Elijah presents himself to Ahab and tells him that the drought is because of Ahab and Jezebel. This is pretty serious stuff. Their god of choice, Baal, is the thunder and rain god.

Elijah prudently disappears. First, some ravens take care of him, then a poor widow, whose son Elijah raises from the dead. Meanwhile, Ahab is scouring the country for the gruff prophet.

At last, Ahab sends out his palace chief Obadiah to look for grass and water for the royal livestock, dying because of the drought. Obadiah encounters Elijah, who tells him to inform the king that Elijah will soon make an appearance. Obadiah's response? Abject fear and a funny monologue asking why Elijah is doing this terrible thing to him—this thing that will most certainly result in his painful death (1 Kings 18).

During the course of his plea (which is about as long as the Sermon on the Mount), Obadiah tells how—in order to spare them from Ahab and Jezebel's pogrom—he once secreted one hundred prophets of the Lord in two caves (fifty to a cave, the author helpfully points out for the benefit of the mathematically challenged among his readers) and provided them with food and water for three years.

Here Beginneth the Digression

This brings up an intriguing scene. Can you visualize fifty mouthy, curmudgeonly old prophets confined in a small, drafty cave for three years? Talk about your constant ego-clash:

"Well, it's clear that I'm the greatest prophet of all. I foresaw this."

"So? I foresaw the Red Sox winning the pennant."

"Did not."

"Did too."

"I knew you were going to say that."

"Did not."

It's also a great premise for a popular TV series—*Survivor Samaria*. Put fifty grumpy prophets in two cramped caves for three years. Hilarity ensues.

Here Endeth the Digression

Finally, Elijah and Ahab do meet up. Ahab says (in a rather off-hand manner), "Is it you, you troubler of Israel?" (18:18). From somebody other than a king, you might take that as a bit of good-natured kidding. But Ahab don't kid.

Elijah fearlessly challenges the king. "Round up the best four hundred fifty prophets of Baal and the top four hundred fifty of Baal's consort Asherah and let's duke it out, once and for all, atop Mount Carmel." Ahab agrees and summons all of the Israelites to watch the spectacle. It's a winner-take-all prophetic grudge match.

Elijah proposes to slaughter two bulls. Each is to be placed on an altar at the top of Mount Carmel. Each side will call on his deity. The winner is the side whose deity consumes the offering in flames. The people of Israel like the idea. This ought to be good.

The prophets of Baal go first. They weep. They wail. They dance. They implore.

Nothing.

About noon, Elijah wanders up and delivers one of the great snappy comebacks in the entire Bible:

"Cry aloud! Surely he is a god; either he is meditating, or he has wandered away, or he is on a journey, or perhaps he is asleep and must be awakened" (1 Kings 18:27).

But here's one of the funny—if faintly off-color—bits. Our sensibilities are so tender that generations of biblical translators have carefully sanitized Elijah's jibes. "Wandered away" is a euphemism for going to the bathroom (which is actually a euphemism for relieving yourself). A tough old bird like Elijah most certainly did not say "wandered away."

You know the rest of the story. The prophets of Baal cut themselves with knives, Baal never shows, the Lord consumes Elijah's sacrifice even after he surrounds it with a trench full of water, and the fickle people of Israel pounce on Baal's four hundred fifty, whereupon Elijah kills them in the Wadi Kishon. Oh yeah, and the drought ends.

Here Beginneth the Digression

The thing is, Elijah's successor Elisha has an even odder sense of humor!

Elijah has been carried away in a whirlwind, and, after a miracle or two of his own, Elisha heads to Bethel. Along the way, a group of teenage boys wander out of the city and begin laughing at him, saying, "Go away, baldhead! Go away, baldhead!" Elisha has a particularly Christian-like response. He calls on the Lord and a couple of "she-bears" lumber out of the hills and maul 42 of the teenagers (2 Kings 2:23-24).

Um, I'm not sure exactly what the author's point is here. Lord knows, all the parents I know have wanted to maul a teenage boy or two in their time (although sending them to a mall instead of mauling them is probably more socially acceptable now), but "Yo, baldie! Beat it!" would appear to be a relatively mild insult, even for someone who is follicley-challenged like Elisha.

Perhaps the point is that it is never a good idea to question the Lord's anointed. Perhaps it was a message to the pagan folk of that area. Or perhaps the message is that this kind of scornful, jeering mocking will get you in big trouble.

(I am curious about the "she-bear" business, though. What's wrong with "he-bears"? Aren't they ferocious enough? Could it be that a taunt like "Yo, baldie!" isn't vicious enough to disturb another male from hibernating or something?)

Here Endeth the Digression

Okay, so the punchline to the prophets of Baal story isn't terribly funny, but Elijah's droll commentary on ol' Baal *is* a great sarcastic put-down. The entire sequence is rife with humor and it doesn't take much imagination to hear it told and retold over Jewish fireplaces over the past few thousand years . . . and to imagine that, in the hands of a master storyteller, it gets funnier with each successive retelling.

Mirth

The other word that at least implies genial good humor and gentle laughter is *mirth*. We've covered laughing/laughter (scornful and otherwise), happy/happiness, and now mirth/mirthyness (as Stephen Colbert might say). There are a dozen references to *mirth* in Strong's, and they paint a somewhat different picture of the O.T. (There are no references to the word *mirth* in the New Testament, incidentally.) Again, the emphasis is mine.

1. Genesis 31:27
We're back in the tense encounter between Jacob and Laban. Laban is chewing Jacob out for slipping away in the middle of the night with his two daughters:
> "Why did you flee secretly and deceive me and not tell me? I would have sent you away with **mirth** and songs, with tambourine and lyre."

2. Nehemiah 8:12
The NRSV doesn't use the word "mirth" here, but the King James does. The exiles have returned to Jerusalem and, under Nehemiah's expert leadership, they've restored the damaged walls of the city:
> And all the people went their way to eat, and to drink, and to send portions, and to make great **mirth**, because they had understood the words that were declared unto them.

3. Psalm 137: 3-4
This is the beautiful psalm where the captives are lamenting their beautiful homeland, even as they sit by the rivers of Babylon:
> For there our captors
>   asked us for songs,
> and our tormentors asked for **mirth**, saying,
>   "Sing us one of the songs of Zion!"
> How could we sing the LORD's song
>   in a foreign land?

4. Proverbs 14:13
Here, in a bit of a switcheroo, the NRSV translates "mirth" as "laughter":
> Even in **laughter** the heart is sad,
> and the end of joy is grief.

5. Ecclesiastes 8:15
The NRSV doesn't use the word "mirth" here, but the King James does:
> Then I commended **mirth**, because a man hath no better thing under the sun, than to eat, and to drink, and to be **merry**: for that shall abide with him of his labour the days of his life, which God giveth him under the sun.

6. Isaiah 24:8
This is a vision of the impending apocalypse:
> The **mirth** of the timbrels is stilled,
> the noise of the jubilant has ceased,
> the **mirth** of the lyre is stilled.

7. Isaiah 24:11
The NRSV doesn't use "mirth" here, but the King James does in this excerpt from an oracle concerning the city of Tyre:
> There is a crying for wine in the streets; all joy is darkened, the **mirth** of the land is gone.

8. Jeremiah 7:34
The Lord (via Jeremiah) promises desolation and despair for the people's disobedience:
> And I will bring to an end the sound of **mirth** and gladness, the voice of the bride and bridegroom in the cities of Judah and in the streets of Jerusalem; for the land shall become a waste.

9. Jeremiah 16:9
The Lord (via Jeremiah) promises still more desolation and despair for the people's disobedience:
> For thus says the LORD of hosts, the God of Israel: I am going to banish from this place, in your days and before your eyes, the voice of **mirth** and the voice of gladness, the voice of the bridegroom and the voice of the bride.

10. Jeremiah 25:10
The Lord (via Jeremiah) promises EVEN MORE desolation and despair for the people's disobedience, using pretty much the same language as before (note to Jeremiah: get a thesaurus):

And I will banish from them the sound of **mirth** and the sound of gladness, the voice of the bridegroom and the voice of the bride, the sound of the millstones and the light of the lamp.

11. Ezekiel 21:9-10

The Lord (via Ezekiel) promises desolation and despair for the people's disobedience:

Mortal, prophesy and say: Thus says the LORD; Say:
A sword, a sword is sharpened,
   it is also polished;
it is sharpened for slaughter,
   honed to flash like lightning!
How can we **make merry?**
   You have despised the rod,
   and all discipline.

12. Hosea 2:11

The Lord (via Hosea this time) promises desolation and despair for the people's disobedience : . . . yadda, yadda, yadda:

I will put an end to all her **mirth**,
   her festivals, her new moons, her sabbaths,
   and all her appointed festivals.

The sum total of these verses is that "mirth" is a *good* thing—and you guys are about to lose it. Normally, you can't have a longing for something that's not desirable, and one of the first things the disobedient Israelites will lose (along with their lives, their land, and their freedom) is the ability to laugh, to enjoy life, to have fun, to experience something we'll talk more about later—joy.

There's more, of course. The entire little book of Jonah is a comedy—and has been called such by more than one scholar, including John Morreall (1999, 95). Esther—the lone book in the Old or New Testaments that doesn't mention God!—can be read as a riotous comedy, according to Lynn Tatum (pers. comm.). Then there's Job, of course, generally thought to be a tragedy. But one of the ways to determine if a story is a comedy or a tragedy is: in a comedy, the hero learns his lesson, and boy! does Job learn his. Plus, he gets all of his stuff back and then some, at the end. Had this been a true tragedy, he would have died a noble, heroic death, unrepentant and unyielding. But he would have been just as dead. (See Shakespeare, William, *Hamlet, Macbeth, Titus Andronicus,* et al.)

Frederick Buechner finds humor in at least one more unlikely place, 1 Kings 10:5. "I challenge anybody to deny that there was at least a smile on the lips of the ancient narrator who wrote that after the Queen of Sheba's staggering tour of King Solomon's palace, 'There was no more spirit in her'" (1979, author's note).

Preach It, Qohelet!

In the end, let's return to the word that started this whole journey, *laughter*. There are two conflicting, but equally compelling, references to laughter in the writings of that old reprobate Qohelet (or the Preacher, although sometimes attributed to King Solomon himself) that we know as Ecclesiastes. As you might imagine for a book with the central theme "all is vanity," this isn't jolly reading. The first references to laughter are definite downers (and trust me here, the emphasis is definitely mine when it comes to Qohelet's words):

> I said to myself, "Come now, I will make a test of pleasure; enjoy yourself." But again, this also was vanity. I said of **laughter**, "It is mad," and of pleasure, "What use is it?" (Ecclesiastes 2:1-2)

> A good name is better than precious ointment,
>   and the day of death, than the day of birth.
> It is better to go to the house of mourning
>   than to go to the house of feasting;
> for this is the end of everyone,
>   and the living will lay it to heart.
> Sorrow is better than **laughter**,
>   for by sadness of countenance the heart is made glad.
> The heart of the wise is in the house of mourning;
>   but the heart of fools is in the house of mirth.
> It is better to hear the rebuke of the wise
>   than to hear the song of fools.
> For like the crackling of thorns under a pot,
>   so is the **laughter** of fools;
>   this also is vanity.
> (Ecclesiastes 7:1-6)

Whoa! Preacher! Lighten up, dude. In the second set of references, the author appears to be telling us that sad is better than glad; that every happiness, every bit of laughter is *always*, inevitably followed by a long period of crushing despair and depression; and if that's the case, then that's good because we only learn stuff when we're miserable.

It's also possible to read this as Qohelet saying that you can't replace sorrow with happiness. They are both with us always, as the two main aspects of the human condition in this cruel, bitter world. Don't get too comfortable and happy because life is about to throw another series of bitter defeats and disappointments any second.

This way of thinking made a lot of sense, especially for much of the history of civilization, when the great mass of people were chronically malnourished, constantly dying as pawns in the wars between kings, and keeling over dead from an array of hideous diseases.

And make no mistake, there is plenty of hunger, war, and illness now. But if you've got enough financial resources to buy this book (instead of spending your last dollar on food or rent), then you're a representative of that tiny fraction of modern humanity who is doing okay. Does this outlook resonate with you today? Is it even appropriate or healthy to have that kind of fatalistic outlook today?

(And if you think Ecclesiastes is a downer, flip on over to Lamentations . . .)

Still, just when you've about written the Preacher off as manic-depressive, there comes this marvelous little song, one that has been treasured by theologians and pop songwriters alike for millennia:

> For everything there is a season, and a time for every matter under heaven:
>   a time to be born, and a time to die;
>   a time to plant, and a time to pluck up what is planted;
>   a time to kill, and a time to heal; . . .
>   a time to weep, and a time to **laugh**;
>   a time to mourn, and a time to dance.
> (Ecclesiastes 3:1-4)

Yes, there are going to be hard, somber times. Yes, there will be death, destruction, and desolation. But there will also be times to laugh and dance. There will be times to enjoy the miracle of a new birth, and to laugh out loud at the abundance of harvest, an abundance that will feed not just your family but a hundred more besides.

That sentiment reappears unexpectedly late in the book as Qohelet compares and contrasts the fate of a people when the rulers follow the Lord and when rulers do not. In a land with God-fearing leaders, he writes:

> Alas for you, O land, when your king is a servant,
>   and your princes feast in the morning!
> Happy are you, O land, when your king is a nobleman,
>   and your princes feast at the proper time—
>   for strength and not for drunkenness!
> Through sloth the roof sinks in,
>   and through indolence the house leaks.
> Feasts are made for **laughter**;
>   wine gladdens life,
>   and money meets every need.
> (Ecclesiastes 10:16-19)

The Preacher then quickly lapses back into his morose recounting of how miserable everything is. But the underlying point remains—

laughter is good, healthy, and even necessary at the right time, under the right conditions.

Here's what I take away from all of that: even the darkest, most forbidding of the Old Testament's writers can't legislate or mandate that joyful laughter be suppressed always. And remember, after Ecclesiastes comes the Song of Solomon, a giddy, rambunctious, sometimes ribald celebration of love in all its many forms!

Ultimately, we don't find a whole lot of the good kind of laughter recounted in the O.T.—but it is there. You just have to look for it and be open for the moments when the writers take a break from the smiting and begetting and cursing, and let droll stories about very real, very human people slip in.

Perhaps there's more in the New Testament . . .

CHAPTER 3

New Testament Humor

"Jesus I know, and Paul I know; but who the heck are you losers?!"
There's a fair amount of laughter elsewhere among these
sketches too, and I'm prepared to have a lot of people say that
it's unseemly at best and, at worst, enough to get me
defrocked. All I can offer by way of defense is that the Bible
itself has a great deal more laughter in it than all those double
columns and black leatherette bindings would lead you to
believe. —Frederick Buechner (1979)

There are many incidents where laughter and humor might have occurred in the New Testament, along with a number of allusions to laughter. But outright, thigh-slapping laughter appears to be in short supply here too.

We've about exhausted the *Strongest Strong's Exhaustive Concordance* for direct mentions of laughter (and its variations) in the Bible, but there are a few left for the New Testament. Alas, most are—once again— laughter of the scornful, sneering kind (as usual, emphasis is mine).

Matthew 9:23-24

The leader of the synagogue has approached Jesus and asked him to come to the leader's house, where his daughter has just died:

> When Jesus came to the leader's house and saw the flute players and the crowd making a commotion, he said, "Go away; for the girl is not dead but sleeping." And they **laughed** at him.

Mark 5:40

The same scene is reported in Mark:

And they **laughed** at him. Then he put them all outside, and took the child's father and mother and those who were with him, and went in where the child was.

Luke 6:21

In this series of blessings and woes, Jesus contrasts the fate of those who follow him with the fate of those who choose not to. This is part of the so-called Sermon on the Plain:

"Blessed are you who are hungry now,
    for you will be filled.
"Blessed are you who weep now,
    for you will **laugh**."

Luke 6:25

Then Jesus turns it around. The next verses compare the fate of those who refuse to follow the Son of Man to that of those who do follow the Son of Man:

"Woe to you who are full now,
    for you will be hungry.
"Woe to you who are **laughing** now,
    for you will mourn and weep."

Luke 8:52-53

The raising of the little girl first reported in Matthew and Mark gets a third retelling in Luke:

They were all weeping and wailing for her; but he said, "Do not weep; for she is not dead but sleeping." And they **laughed** at him.

James 4:7-10

James has just condemned, in the strongest possible words, various (and apparently fairly common) disputes among Christians. He attacks people who are "friends" with the world, who have chosen accommodation to the secular society around them. He next goes after the "proud," and calls for humility among his readers. At last, James gives sound counsel to all those involved in sinful behavior:

Submit yourselves therefore to God. Resist the devil, and he will flee from you. Draw near to God, and he will draw near to you. Cleanse your hands, you sinners, and purify your hearts, you double-minded. Lament and mourn and weep. Let your **laughter** be turned into mourning and your joy into dejection. Humble yourselves before the Lord, and he will exalt you.

Of these, the most intriguing is the Luke 6 passage, in part because Jesus says this just before the "love your enemies" bit. This is Jesus' first sermon to his newly assembled apostles and it is a radically new way of thinking, an earth-shifting way of looking at things. It's the first charge to the twelve disciples . . . and laughter is part of it! This introductory sermon turns everything the apostles thought they knew about the world and the way of the world upside down.

I like to think Jesus delivered the entire list of blessings and woes with a sometimes mischievous smile, not really a sermon per se, but more of a gentle sharing with the people he loved. It's like poetry— it's easy to imagine him enjoying the cadences of the language, enjoying surprising people (this is the "love your enemy" talk), enjoying the time together. Did some of the people in the crowd chuckle at some of these wonderfully contradictory sayings? I would hazard a guess they did. Did he laugh during all of this? I have to believe so.

SO THIS PHARISEE WITH A LOG IN HIS EYE SAYS, "WOULD YOU LIKE TO DANCE WITH ME?" AND HIS DATE SAYS, "WOULD I, WOULD I?!"

JESUS DOES STAND-UP

Blessed *and* Happy

Still, that's a pretty short list of instances of the actual word "laugh." If we're still in agreement that being "happy" at least sometimes means that a person is doing a *little* laughing, then we can expand the pool somewhat, but not in the New Revised Standard Version. The King James translation, however, substitutes the word *happy* for *blessed* in several places, including (emphasis mine, naturally):

John 13:16-17:
> Verily, verily, I say unto you, The servant is not greater than his lord; neither he that is sent greater than he that sent him. If ye know these things, **happy** are ye if ye do them.

Romans 14:22:
> Hast thou faith? have it to thyself before God. **Happy** is he that condemneth not himself in that thing which he alloweth.

James 5:11:
> Behold, we count them **happy** which endure. Ye have heard of the patience of Job, and have seen the end of the Lord; that the Lord is very pitiful, and of tender mercy.

1 Peter 3:14:
> But and if ye suffer for righteousness' sake, **happy** are ye: and be not afraid of their terror, neither be troubled.

1 Peter 4:14:
> If ye be reproached for the name of Christ, **happy** are ye; for the spirit of glory and of God resteth upon you: on their part he is evil spoken of, but on your part he is glorified.

Mirth Out; Mire In?

The other word that at least implies the possibility for humor and laughter is *mirth*. Alas, *Strong's* (2001) says there are more references to "miry," as in "the miry clay" (4) than there are references to "mirth" (0).

There is at least one other veiled reference that may or may not refer to something akin to humor in Ephesians 5:4:

Entirely out of place is obscene, silly, and vulgar talk; but instead, let there be thanksgiving.

Well, that settles it, right? Humor is out.

As usual, however, the context is something a little deeper. Ephesians 5:3 and 5:5 refer specifically to sexual impurity. New Testament scholar David Garland tells me that the Greek noun *eutrapelia* (particularly in this context) refers not so much to jesting (as the KJV translates it) but "coarse joking, suggestive overtones, double entendres"—generally about sex (more on this in chapter 4).

There are glimmers of humor, particularly in the Gospels. Some writers have observed that the closer the writers of the Gospel are to the life of Jesus, the more likely there is at least *some* implied humor in Jesus' life. By that measure, Mark has the most, Luke and Matthew next, then John. Conversely, the further they are from the events of his life, the less the humor potential (Trueblood 1964, 19).

A similar example is when the producers of the movie *Gandhi* began pre-production, Indian officials initially wanted Gandhi shown only as a beam of light, not a real live human—and one known to have laughed regularly!

To modern eyes, when reading to purposely *exclude the possibility of humor*—as most of us have been trained to do—there just isn't much lighthearted material in the New Testament.

Does this mean the N.T. is . . . well . . . a bit *testy?* Not when you consider that the best humor is *not* in jokes. The most robust laughter does not come from puns. Genuine humor is—as we saw in chapter 1—the natural offshoot of putting interesting people into challenging situations and listening to their responses. Humor that endures flows from character, not from witty wordplay or slapstick.

Seen through that lens, there are numerous places in the New Testament rich in humorous potential. While Trueblood found them primarily in Mark, I seem to run across more such situations in Matthew. Let's examine some of them.

Aiming Up Always Works

Matthew 2:12-16

As we've seen, one of the basic tenets of humor is that it operates better upward. Poking fun at the foibles of the powerful is funny.

Poking fun at the weak and less fortunate is bullying. Everybody likes to see the mighty made fun of.

Even though he is Rome's poodle, Herod is a bloodthirsty dictator, paranoid and brutal. The Jews hate Herod's ham-fisted rule. And when he hears that a child will be born during his watch, a child who will someday become more powerful than he, Herod flies into a murderous rage.

It is then that a handful of wise men (some have suggested they may have been priests from Parthia, Rome's long-time adversary) arrive in his capitol looking for the child who would be king. It's not surprising that Herod's evil little mind quickly begins to work overtime. He summons the wise men to his court and purrs, "When you find him, let me know—I'd like to pay . . . um, *homage* . . . to the little guy, too!"

But these priests aren't called "wise men" for nothing. They do, indeed, locate the Holy Family and leave their baby shower gifts. But they've been warned in a dream not to report back to Herod, and instead they slip out via the back roads. Herod, no doubt, is absolutely furious.

Once again, it doesn't much imagination to think that word of Herod getting outfoxed swept like wildfire through the ranks of his courtiers, hangers-on, minions, and lackeys . . . and out into the Jewish countryside. Powdered court officials and humble Hebrew shepherds alike probably got a good laugh out of that one . . . very, very privately and quietly, of course.

Even the Romans probably heard about it and snickered, which probably enraged Herod most of all.

The Power of Surprise

Matthew 14:24-33

Of all the disciples, none places himself in potentially funny positions more often than headstrong, slightly vain Peter. You've got to love a guy who is so eager to be liked—think of a six-month-old golden retriever puppy—but whose enthusiasm is always causing problems.

When we pick up this story thread, we've already seen a *serious* manifestation of Jesus' power—the feeding of the five thousand. The terrified disciples have been knocked around the little wave-tossed boat all night long. In the morning, Jesus nonchalantly walks towards them. At first, they think it is a ghost, but Jesus quickly identifies himself.

Peter, in typically impetuous fashion, is the first to react.

"Lord!" he shouts, "If it is you, command me to come to you on the water."

"Come," Jesus says.

And Peter does. He bounds over the side and begins walking toward Jesus. No one is more amazed than Peter. My guess is he preens a bit—shooting a smug glance over his shoulder at the other disciples. But the storm is still raging and, when a fierce wind nearly knocks him off his feet, Peter loses faith. Immediately, he sinks, shouting, "Lord, save me!"

Jesus is there. He hauls Peter out of the sea and—together, I think—they walk to the little boat. "You of little faith," he whispers, "why did you doubt?" Immediately, the storm stills. (One nice touch is that Jesus says "little faith"—not "no faith." Remember—the other eleven were all passively watching this little drama, none of them were willing to get their feet wet.)

The humor comes first from Peter's puppy-dog enthusiasm, followed by his unceremonious dunking. And again, I wouldn't be surprised to discover someday that he was the butt of plenty of ribbing by the other guys in the days that followed. But at least Peter tried . . .

Matthew 15:21-28 and Mark 7:24-28

Another persistent character in the Jesus narratives is the unnamed Canaanite woman in Matthew 15 (identified as a Gentile in Mark). She pleads with Jesus to heal her demon-possessed daughter. He, at first (apparently), ignores her, and then engages in this curious dialogue:

"I was sent only to the lost sheep of the house of Israel."

She's not dissuaded. She humbles herself before him and says, "Lord, help me."

"It is not fair to take the children's food and throw it to the dogs," he responds.

"Yes, Lord, yet even the dogs eat the crumbs that fall from their masters' table."

Jesus is pleased—this entire exchange has obviously been for the benefit of the Twelve and all of the others who have been following him.

"Woman, great is your faith! Let it be done for you as you wish."

And her daughter is healed.

This isn't funny *ha ha*. This is funny ironic. First, Jesus asks his audience to love their neighbors. "Sure," they say, "we love 'em, Lord." Then he puts a face on a *neighbor* . . . a hated Canaanite. He's saying, "Okay, now, all you elitists who believe you're the only folks who are going to heaven . . . watch this!"

Who is laughing here? Maybe only Jesus. If humor is about surprise—and it is—then there are a whole bunch of people in the audience that day who are flat-out stunned. Jesus loves shaking people's preconceptions and misconceptions. With the help of a tenacious Canaanite woman, he's able to do just that.

I'm guessing he's smiling the whole time . . . both at the woman, to let her know that he's actually encouraging her during this pivotal bit of dialogue . . . and at the discomfort of some of the "righteous" people in the crowd. *And* he gets to heal a child.

Not bad for a single lesson!

Surprise + Aiming Up = More Power

Matthew 17:24-27

There are certain moments in the New Testament that display Jesus' whimsical side. It seems to me that he sometimes uses humor to defuse a potentially dangerous situation, as he does here. Jesus and his merry band have reached Capernaum, where the tax collectors are busy, busy, busy collecting both the Roman taxes and the Jewish temple tax. The only people who are exempt are priests, rabbis, and—of course—the royal families. But the tax collectors are puzzled. Is Jesus a rabbi? Lots of people seem to think so. So they send a delegation to Peter. "Does Jesus pay the temple tax?" "Yes," Peter says.

Later, when Peter has related the incident to Jesus, Jesus does something curious.

"Okay, Peter, what do you think about this?" he asks. "For instance, do the children of kings have to cough up taxes?"

For once, an easy question! "Nope," Peter responds.

Jesus nods. "So their children are free."

"Yup."

As usual, a large crowd has gathered, including collectors of the temple tax (by and large honorable Jews) and probably collectors of the Roman taxes (by and large, not so honorable). Jesus doesn't want to embarrass the Jews, nor is he ready to provoke the Romans—at least, not yet. And here's where the magic and whimsy come in.

"Peter, since we don't want to offend anybody, go down to the sea, throw out a hook, and reel in the first fish you catch. In its mouth, you'll find a coin that will cover *both* of our temple taxes."

That's exactly what happens—Pete hauls in a giant catfish and in its mouth is the coin. Naturally, the crowd laughs and applauds.

A couple of things are happening here. First, Jesus is subtly asserting that God's in control, not Rome. He and Peter will pay the tax (and this will come up again), but it will be under *his* terms and not from *their* common treasury. Second, he avoids a tense situation and lets everybody off the hook (literally!) by making this a lighthearted incident. Sure, he could have pretended to have found the coin on the ground or in a flower. Heck, Jesus could have pulled it from behind someone's ear. But by using something silly like a fish to make a serious statement, Jesus makes every moment a Teaching Moment.

Matthew 22:1-10 and Luke 14:15-24

This is the parable of the wedding banquet—and we'll see it again in the pages ahead. And if Jesus' onlookers and rubberneckers were blindsided by the previous sermon illustration, this one knocks 'em on their *burkhas*. A great king throws a lavish feast for all of the rich and powerful and sends out servants with invitations. But the hoi polloi not only diss the king, they mistreat his servants. Jesus saves the best (or worst) excuse for last—"I have just been married, and therefore I cannot come." Really! Infuriated, the king sends the surviving servants out to find society's outcasts and untouchables and feeds them the rich food of the banquet.

It's likely that there was shocked silence at the end of this parable, interrupted only by the sound of jaws dropping. At this day and time, this story was unthinkable! Again, I can see Jesus smiling. He'd overturned another applecart.

Exaggeration

Perhaps the most common scenario in which to imagine a smiling Jesus is when he uses exaggeration for both comic effect and to make a serious point. Some places that may have happened:

Matthew 7:3 and Luke 6:41

Jesus tells the hypocrite to get the log out of his own eye before he condemns the mote of dust in his neighbor's eye.

Matthew 7:9-10 and Luke 11:11-12

Jesus asks what parent will give a child a stone or a serpent's egg when that child asks for a piece of bread.

Matthew 19:24, Mark 10:25, and Luke 18:25

It's easier, Jesus observes, for a camel to squeeze through the eye of a needle than it is for a rich person to get to heaven. Or, as revisited by Frederick Buechner: It is "easier for Nelson Rockefeller to pass through the night deposit slot of the Chase Manhattan Bank would seem to me a reasonable modern equivalent" (1979, author's note).

In each of these instances, I think we can make the case that Jesus is using dramatic language for maximum impact. Responses to these statements doubtless range from horrified denial to slow, spreading smiles on the faces of those who see where the Master is heading. These are vivid, unforgettable images that still resonate two thousand years later.

Mixing Styles Works Too

Luke 18:1-8

A different kind of story with a different kind of smile-inducing humor is to be found in Luke 18, the parable of the judge and the persistent widow. In a day when widows had few rights, this one woman bravely refuses to accept her fate. She badgers an unjust judge ceaselessly until, at last, in exasperation (although in his words there is possibly a muted hint of admiration at her dogged determination), the judge finally gives her what she desires. (Perhaps it would help here to imagine Alec Guinness as the unjust judge and Rosie O'Donnell as the nagging, relentless widow.) Regardless, Jesus' use of exaggeration, juxtaposition, and shock makes its point. Does the judge smile when he wearily grants Rosie justice? It makes the story—in my mind, anyway—richer to think so. Does Jesus smile when he reaches the surprise ending? I rather think so . . .

Luke 13:31-32

We know Jesus could get angry (the cleansing of the temple, calling the Pharisees "white-washed tombs"), but could Jesus be wryly sardonic—or even (gasp!) a little sarcastic?

Take another look at Luke 13:31-32. Late in his ministry, while Jesus is preaching and healing, a group of Pharisees armed with inside information warn Jesus to flee; Herod is looking for him with murderous intent.

Jesus says, "Go and tell that *fox* for me, 'Listen, I am casting out demons and performing cures today and tomorrow, and on the third day I finish my work'" (emphasis mine, of course).

This is another example that Jesus is fearless, of course. But it also has a tinge of wry humor. Why a fox? They're crafty and sly—but they hide from people and larger animals, skulking around the periphery, hoping to score an easy meal. The image of the pompous, bejeweled Herod as a skulking fox, oppressing Jews even has he cowers before Rome, most assuredly elicited gasps and stifled giggles from those present. Jesus is issuing both a challenge and a prophecy. Herod will have his part to play, but only Jesus knows at the time that mighty Herod will be but a bit player in the great cosmic drama to come.

John 1:35-51

Another scene that seems ripe with comic potential is the encounter with those who will become Jesus' first disciples following his baptism by John. Jesus has already called Andrew, Simon Peter, and Philip. Philip finds Nathanael improbably sprawled out under a fig tree and urges him to join the group:

"We have found him about whom Moses in the law and also the prophets wrote, Jesus son of Joseph from Nazareth."

You've gotta love Nathanael's response—he's from the Palestinian equivalent of Missouri; they will have to show him. He says, "Can anything good come out of Nazareth?" Substitute "Waco" or "Brooklyn" or "Hackensack" or "Lodi" in modern times and you get the idea.

Still, Nathanael follows Philip to where Jesus sits under a tree. Even as Nathanael approaches, Jesus calls out, "Here is truly an Israelite in whom there is no deceit!"

Nathanael asks, "Um, do we know each other?"

Jesus smiles—how else could he say what he's about to say?— "Friend, I knew you *long* before Philip called for you under that fig tree." And he did.

No fool he, Nathanael drops to his knees. "Teacher, you really are the Son of God! The King of Kings!"

And this is where—by all the laws of human nature, common sense, and everything we know about our loving Lord and Savior tells us— Jesus MUST have laughed. He says, "You believe all of that just because I told you I saw you before you were under the fig tree?! Ha! Friend, you ain't seen *nothing* yet! Stick around and you're going to see bigger things than that. And someday soon, you're going to see heaven open and angels parading to earth celebrating the Son of Man!"

I'm guessing Jesus laughs happily and even gives Nathanael a big ol' bear hug.

And before long, Nathanael gathers his wits and he's laughing, too.

What a ride they're about to embark on together!

Points of Greatest Potential

Two particularly poignant moments in the Gospels seem to me to have the greatest potential for laughter from our Savior.

John 2:1-11

The first takes place at the wedding in Cana, which also records Jesus' first miracle. The story occurs after the call of the first disciples, and it is one of the seminal events in Jesus' ministry. Buechner loves this story as well—he says there is a "curious luminousness" about the event:

> [W]hat we carry from it most powerfully is simply a feeling for the joy
> of it—a wedding that almost flopped except that this strange, stern
> guest came and worked a miracle and it turned out to be the best
> wedding of all. Certainly it is because of the joy of it that it is remem-
> bered in the marriage service. (1969, 90–91)

Weddings are generally joyful occasions anyway, but this one is about to be spoiled—they're about to run out of wine! The wedding planner, the wine steward, and the caterer are coming to blows, the bridegroom's mom is blaming the bridegroom's dad, and the bride's parent never really liked the no-account groom anyhow. Mary the mother of Jesus finds him in a corner, and he reluctantly agrees to help. Jesus transforms six massive stone water jars into wine. The wine steward doubtfully takes a sip, and then a broad smile splits his face.

"Yowsa!" he shouts to the wedding party. "Listen, everybody! At most parties, people serve the good stuff first, then roll out the cheap white wine in cardboard boxes after folks are a little tipsy. Not here!" He grabs the bridegroom around the neck and gives him noogies. "No sir, not here! This knucklehead saved the good—no, the *great*—wine for now!"

Like any good Jewish wedding, singing and dancing, eating and drinking, and general merrymaking follow long into the night. You can't tell me that the first disciples, the few servants in the know, and Mary and Jesus didn't share a few secret smiles or bust out laughing at some point during the evening. They know what really happened in Cana that night. Jesus lets the confused bridegroom take the props— but this is just too much fun. If Jesus *didn't* laugh here, it would have been plain unnatural.

Luke 19:1-10

The second poignant moment, and the final place in the Gospels where—it seems to me—there is an element of humor and mirth, is the well-known story of Zacchaeus. It is particularly interesting because, at least according to Luke, it is the final event before the Passion narrative begins.

One day, Jesus and his retinue pass through Jericho. They've been hounded every step of the way by the Pharisees and scribes. People love a good fight, so the crowds show up to watch the fireworks.

Among the faces in the mob is Zacchaeus, a vertically-challenged tax collector. Zacchaeus collected Rome's duties and, not surprisingly, he was hated by the Jews. Whenever Zacchaeus tried to press forward to see Jesus, the crowd bunched together tighter to squeeze him out. No doubt a few stray cuffs and kicks were directed his way too. Tax collectors were probably fair game.

At last, Zacchaeus shinnies up a handy sycamore tree where he's got a better view. Tax collectors typically eat well and sycamores aren't the stoutest of trees, by the way. So it's at that moment, as he sways precariously above the crowd, that Jesus sees him.

"Zacchaeus, hurry and come down; for I must stay at your house today."

If Zacchaeus is flabbergasted, the mob is mad. They hate the fat little tax collector—and all of a sudden they're not all that wild about Jesus, either.

Zacchaeus collects himself, overcome with emotion. "Look, half of my possessions, Lord, I will give to the poor; and if I have defrauded anyone of anything, I will pay back four times as much."

Now it is time for Jesus to smile broadly. "Today salvation has come to this house, because he too is a son of Abraham. For the Son of Man came to seek out and to save the lost."

The crowd's reaction isn't recorded (although they probably didn't shower Zacchaeus with roses), but while he has their attention, Jesus launches into the parable of the ten pounds (Luke 19:11-27). When he finishes, Jesus departs immediately for his fateful entry into Jerusalem. Obviously, this is a pivotal moment.

The jewel-like little scene contains elements of several different kinds of laughter. While the crowd may laugh derisively to see the hated Zacchaeus dangling from a sycamore, Jesus may laugh with happiness. He loves to see people approach him innocently, eagerly—like children.

When Jesus says, "Zacchaeus, come on down, friend. You're about to buy me lunch," there is even more bitter laughter and muttering in the assembled multitude. "Jesus is eating with a sinner—one of those bloodsucking Roman parasites who milk us dry!"

But that sniping is trumped by Zacchaeus's excited proclamation—made all the more impressive when you know that tax collectors routinely bilk the Jews. No doubt Zacchaeus pulls out all the stops for dinner too.

As for Jesus, his quiet chuckling may have erupted into outright laughter at this point. He knows what's in the hearts of those who watch this entire scenario play out, "How come that dirty little turncoat Zacchaeus? Why not me? I'm a good guy." Perhaps some of them *are* "good" people.

But it's more important to Jesus that he's just seen another soul saved, a man hated and despised by an entire community, just the kind of scapegoat the Master particularly loves. Even the lavish nature of Zacchaeus's apparent confession and gift makes the Savior laugh.

Remember the parable of the banquet—it's the outcasts, losers, and sinners who will someday feast at the Master's table!

The Rest of the New Testament

Like the Old Testament, the rest of the New Testament doesn't present much readily apparent humor or humor potential. That's not its point, after all. Outside of Acts and Revelation (which may have the least laughs of any book in the Bible except Numbers or one of the minor prophets), most of the remainder of the N.T. was written by Paul and other early church leaders, usually letters to specific churches with specific instructions for specific crises and questions. There's usually not a lot of opportunity for lightheartedness in instructions and reproof.

Paul doesn't have much to say about the person of Jesus, either. That makes sense, though, when you realize that Paul's letters were written and circulated among the tiny new churches decades before the Gospels were codified—meaning that we probably know as much about the life of Christ as Paul did. Did Jesus laugh? Our dour friend Mr. Paul (aka Saul) probably isn't the right guy to ask.

That pretty well leaves the Acts of the Apostles, the last bit of history in the Bible. And when you've got history, you've got the opportunity for a smile or two, even if it is inadvertent.

Acts 12:1-19

Like much humor, this story juxtaposes tragedy with comedy. King Herod Agrippa I (the grandson of the original Herod the Great, a chip off granddad's murderous block) is persecuting the new Christians and has executed James, the brother of John. He orders Peter arrested and thrown in a dungeon, bound by double chains. The People of the Way respond the only way they know how—they pray.

The night before his execution, surrounded by guards, Peter's sleep is disturbed by an angel who nudges him awake. "We gotta go, Rocky," the angel whispers, and the chains fall off Peter's wrists. Peter obviously is a bit foggy here, having had his REMs interrupted.

"Um, put on your belt and sandals," the angel prompts.

Peter nods and does so. "Man, this dream seems so real," he thinks.

"Peter, go ahead and put on your coat too," the angel continues, "and follow me."

"Right. My coat."

Finally dressed appropriately, Peter and the angel walk past two sets of guards, and the prison's iron gates swing open for them.

It's not until they are safely away that the angel disappears and Peter realizes that this is not, in fact, a dream.

He heads post-hastily to the large house of Mary, mother of John Mark, where his friends are still praying for him. This is where the author of Acts allows for a little more comic relief.

Peter knocks at the outer gate. Finally, the maid Rhoda appears.

"Rhoda!" Peter hisses, "Let me in! It's me, Peter!"

Rhoda is so dumbfounded; she leaves Peter standing outside, shivering and expecting the furious Roman guards to come pounding around the corner any second. She runs to the den and shouts that Peter is standing at the outer gate! He's free!

The bleary-eyed house party says, "Yeah, sure. Peter. Free. You are one crazy little maid, Rhoda."

The biblical account adds this droll little detail:

> Meanwhile Peter continued knocking; and when they opened the
> gate, they saw him and were amazed. He motioned to them with his
> hand to be silent, and described for them how the Lord had brought
> him out of the prison. And he added, "Tell this to James and to the
> believers." (vv. 16-17)

And after all of that, Peter leaves and spends the night elsewhere (no
doubt as far away from Rhoda as possible).

Alas, Herod the Grandson shares his grandfather's malady—he doesn't
have a sense of humor, either. He promptly lowers the boom on all of
the hapless guards.

Barbara Reid says that Rhoda's misadventure has much in common
with the Greco-Roman stories of that era, popular comedies where wit-
less slaves spend much of the play running around, bungling important
messages and generally causing havoc. *"Meanwhile,"* the text emphasizes, Peter (who is really nervous by now) continues nervously knock-
ing away like a madman. Good stuff (2003, 1979).

Acts 19:11-16

If the previous scene plays out like an outtake from the movie *A
Funny Thing Happened on the Way to the Forum*, this next bit of business
could have come from *Buffy the Vampire Slayer*. Our buddy Paul is in
Ephesus and the power of the Holy Spirit is mightily upon him. Even
handkerchiefs and aprons that he touches are healing people of dis-
ease and demon possession. (I'm guessing here that these *aren't* the
kinds of aprons you see on weekend suburban dads, grilling rib eyes in
the backyard—aprons that say things like "Friends don't let friends
drink White Zinfandel" or "Emeril is my homeboy.")

One day, a group of "itinerant Jewish exorcists" shows up, the seven
sons of the Jewish high priest Sceva. They try to get into the act, casting out evil spirits by proclaiming, "I adjure you by the Jesus whom Paul
proclaims" (v. 13).

Jesus' name is so potent, that the seven actually summon up a
demon in a man! The demon-possessed man stands before the seven
quaking brothers and booms in a big voice, like James Earl Jones, "Jesus
I know, and Paul I know; but who the heck are you losers?!"

When they don't have a real good answer, the demon/man pounces
on them and kicks some serious itinerant Jewish exorcist hiney! He

whups up on them so bad that all seven stagger into the street, bleed-ing, bruised, and naked as jaybirds. The next day everybody in Ephesus has heard the story.

Here Beginneth the Digression

It's presidential election season, and craggy, crusty old Senator Lloyd Bentsen of Texas is the Democratic vice presidential nominee, facing Senator Dan Quayle, his much younger Republican counterpart. Quayle's youth naturally becomes an issue during the campaign, and, at one point during a televised debate, Quayle protests that he's about the same age as John F. Kennedy and has had as much experience as JFK had when he was elected pres-ident.

Bentsen doesn't miss a beat.

"Senator," Bentsen drawls, "I served with Jack Kennedy; I knew Jack Kennedy; Jack Kennedy was a friend of mine. Senator, you are no Jack Kennedy" (October 5, 1988).

If nothing else, this proves that Senator Bentsen proba-bly read the book of Acts at least once.

Here Endeth the Digression

It's a funny enough scene on its own, but with a serious underpin-ning. There is, indeed, *power* in the name of Jesus. One of my favorite cartoons (by Mark Sisson) has Jesus standing outside a tomb with two heavily bandaged bodies standing expectantly in front of him. Jesus says, "Well, I'm sorry Mr. Lazzowitz, but I *did* specifically say, 'Lazarus, come forth.' "

The next time you see one of those televangelist charlatans blithely using the name of Jesus and selling "holy prayer cloths," remember what happened to the sons of Sceva, seven boys who dabbled in some-thing infinitely more powerful than themselves and barely escaped with their lives.

Acts 20:7-12

This story includes one of the great pratfalls of recorded history. Paul is now in Troas and a serious preaching "jones" is on him—he goes on and on, well past midnight in an upstairs room. A young fellow named Eutychus (whose name, believe it or not, means "Lucky") heroically tries to stay awake through it all, but eventually falls asleep, and promptly topples out of the window where he's been sitting. He smacks the ground three stories below and is dead as a doornail.

Okay, okay, senseless death generally isn't the stuff great comedies are made of, but stay with me here. Paul finds Lucky, nonchalantly brings him back to life, goes back to testifying, and continues strong until dawn. Verse 12 then reads, "Meanwhile they had taken the boy away alive and were not a little comforted." Well, *duh*. As for Eutychus, while *they* may have been comforted, *he* was probably "not a little" confused. "Hey! Why do I have this splitting headache—and where did this sudden fear of heights come from?"

Acts 22:24–23:10

The final bit of at least amusing business involves some verbal magic with the ruling Jewish council, pitting the Sadducees against the Pharisees. The whole event is very much like the clever kid who—while in trouble himself—brings up a sore spot between his parents and slips out unpunished in the ensuing chaos.

Paul has been taken into custody, yet again, and is in the process of being flogged with leather thongs. This can't be a good thing. At last, Paul plays his final trump card. He tells the centurion that he's a Roman citizen and that Rome does not look kindly on its citizens being brutally beaten without due legal process. (Why Paul waited until the flogging was well under way to share this particular little tidbit has always been a mystery to me.) The centurion blanches and orders Paul released.

The next day, the centurion orders Paul to stand before a court comprised of the chief priest and the entire Jewish council, including the old reptile Ananias, who was partially responsible for Jesus' death. Paul soon discovers that this kangaroo court only wants his blood. He sees that there are both Pharisees and Sadducees on the council. Thinking quickly, he allies himself with the Pharisees:

"Brothers, I am a Pharisee, a son of Pharisees. I am on trial concerning the hope of the resurrection of the dead" (v. 6).

Immediately, like modern-day Republicans and Democrats, a fierce debate ensues. The Sadducees did not believe that the dead were someday resurrected, while the Pharisees did. (The Sadducees also favored tax cuts for the rich and sending more chariots to the war in Babylon.) So the Sadducees verbally attack Paul, forcing the Pharisees to defend him. The debate degenerates into violence and the tribune, fearing for Paul's safety, orders the Roman soldiers to hustle him off to the barracks.

It's a dangerous gambit, but Paul was clearly out of options. Still, the courtroom scene is funny in its own way—the whole "enemy of my enemy is my friend" concept is right out of *Alice in Wonderland*. Actually, a *lot* of people were shouting "Off with his head" to Paul in those days.

The Face of a Christian

And that's about it. For all of the glorious preaching, storytelling, parables, prophesy, and instruction, the New Testament just doesn't say much about or even leave many opportunities for humor or laughter. I maintain it was there—Jesus on the road with that wacky band of bumbling disciples was probably the source of long nights of laughter, camaraderie, and deep, deep affection. But specific instances of that very thing are, sadly, all too rare.

Still, I take comfort in Matthew 6:16 (um, yes, the emphasis is mine):

> And whenever you do fast, **do not look dismal**, like the hypocrites, for they disfigure their faces so as to show others that they are fasting. Truly I tell you, they have received their reward.

At the risk of proof-texting, the words "do not look dismal" imply to me that the writers of the New Testament valued a joyous, laughter-filled life, one spent in service to Jesus Christ, lately of Nazareth and storyteller nonpareil. Looking with love at the world, looking serenely happy, content in the knowledge that your future is assured, looking through eyes that reflect the peace that passes all understanding, this is the face of a Christian. In this kind of face, one that reflects the love of Jesus, happiness and laughter would—it seems to me—bubble up uncontrollably.

At least one legendary Christian author, Harry Emerson Fosdick, bought this argument. In *The Manhood of the Master*, Fosdick argued persuasively that the Gospels "clearly" support the belief that the life and teaching of the Christ compel us to believe that: "this joyousness of

Jesus overflowed in all the familiar ways that everywhere are the signs of a radiant nature." Fosdick claimed that "none but a joyful soul" could have loved children, nature, and teaching as Jesus did. He called Jesus' teaching a "spontaneous play of good humor" (Fosdick 1915, 15–16).

And finally, Fosdick—this was back in 1915, mind you—had the audacity to assert that during Jesus' lifetime everyone saw these qualities in the Christ on a daily basis:

> Jesus must have been the most radiant man to be found in his day in Palestine. He must have carried with him an atmosphere of glad good-will. Like springs of fresh water by the sea, even when the salt waves of sorrow went over him, he must have come up again with inexhaustible kindliness and joy. What the gospels report once, must have been his characteristic effect on all who loved him, "Then were the disciples glad when they saw the Lord." (17)

As we shall see in the next chapter, however, it will take nearly two thousand years for Christianity to come to anything like a similar conclusion.

As for Jesus, well . . .

> Joy, which was the small publicity of the pagan, is the gigantic secret of the Christian. And as I close this chaotic volume I open again with the strange small book from which all Christianity came; and I am again haunted by a kind of confirmation. The tremendous figure which fills the Gospels towers in this respect, as in every other, above all the thinkers who ever thought themselves tall. His pathos was natural, almost casual. The Stoics, ancient and modern, were proud of concealing their tears. He never concealed His tears; He showed them plainly on His open face at any daily sight, such as the far sight of His native city. Yet He concealed something. Solemn supermen and imperial diplomatists are proud of restraining their anger. He never restrained His anger. He flung furniture down the front steps of the Temple, and asked men how they expected to escape the damnation of Hell. Yet He restrained something. I say it with reverence; there was in that shattering personality a thread that must be called shyness. There was something that He hid from all men when He went up a mountain to pray. There was something that He covered constantly by abrupt silence or impetuous isolation. There was some one thing that was too great for God to show us when He walked upon our earth; and I have sometimes fancied that it was His mirth. (Chesterton 1909, 296–97)

CHAPTER 4

How the Church Lost the Ability to Laugh

Creator—A comedian whose audience is afraid to laugh.
—H. L. Mencken (1949)

While there is room for honest doubt as to whether or not the Bible forbids, discourages, ignores, or even supports the very human propensity to laughter and mirth, there is no mistaking the beliefs of most well-known Christian theologians and writers in the 2,000 years that followed it.

They *hated* it.

How could/how did Robert Barclay, John Angell James, John Chrysostom, St. Augustine, Thomas Hobbes, William Prynne, and a host of other religious heavy hitters come to such an adamant conclusion?

> This Christian dualism was more optimistic than biblical monism, at least for those who would go to heaven, and in that way, was pro-comic. But in another way, dualism worked against the comic vision, by making the human body into something base, something that opposed what a human being really was, something to be transcended. That evaluation, which had started with St. Paul, was behind the championing of celibacy, Christian monasticism, and later Puritanism, all of which were anti-comic. (Morreall 1999, 112)

Curiously, the contemporaries of the authors of the Old and New Testaments had no such injunctions against laughter and mirth. The surviving records from those ancient cultures are rife with examples of what a modern reader would consider good, old-fashioned slapstick, satire, and humor.

Ancient Egypt

In search of humor, *The Anchor Bible Dictionary* conducts an extensive survey of Egyptian monumental art (including a scene on the tomb of Menna where two girls pull each other's hair), graffiti and racy illustrated papyri, commercial texts from throughout Egypt's long history (including the famed "Satire on the Trades") and literature (the delightfully named King Snofru is comically distracted by women rowers wearing nothing but nets). While there's nothing as immediately accessible as Steve Martin singing (and miming) "King Tut," it seems pretty clear there was some laughter in the Nile delta (Meltzer 1992, 3:326–28).

Mesopotamia

Humor of all kinds, from scatological to profound, abounds in both Sumerian and Akkadian literature and artwork. There is comedy here involving the lowliest animals, soldiers, kings, and the highest gods. Even the legendary tale of Gilgamesh features satire, parody, and unexpected snatches of humor (Foster 1992, 3:328–30). One funny exchange, between a manic-depressive nobleman and his creatively fawning servant seems right out of Shakespeare (Lambert 1960, 139–49):

Master: Servant, listen to me!
Servant: Yes, master, yes!
Master: I will fall in love with a woman.
Servant: [So], fall in love, master, fall in love! The man who falls in love with a woman forgets sorrow and care.
Master: No, servant, I will certainly not fall in love with a woman.
Servant: [Do not] fall in love, master, do not fall in love. A woman is a pitfall, a hole, a ditch; a woman is a sharp iron dagger that slashes a man's throat.

While the writers and assemblers of the modern O.T. were probably not aware of what passed for humor in the rest of the world (Tatum, pers. comm.), it appears that the composers and compilers of what would be called the New Testament most certainly were. Paul was a Roman citizen, Luke apparently spoke and wrote in fluent Greek and the New Testament makes frequent allusions to both civilizations.

Here lies the son of Battus.
He knew well the art of poesy
And how in season to combine
Friendly laughter with his wine. (Callimachus, n/d)

Greece and Rome

In Greece, both comedy and tragedy emerged out of the ancient sacred rituals and services that eventually became part of urban culture. In Athens, in fact, the custom was to present tragedies in the morning and save the comedies for the afternoon (Morreall 1999, 3). Well-known Greek and Roman philosophers, including Aristotle, Plato, Cicero and Quintilian, reference humor and laughter often and widely (Gilhus 1997, 44–45).

So it is possible that at least some of admonitions against laughter and humor in the New Testament are in response to the perceived frivolity of the major competing religions of the day. For example, Gilhus cites the examples of the cults of Dionysus, Demeter, and Aphrodite in ancient Greece, all of which heavily featured laughter. He notes that the tales of the Greek gods are rife with humor and laughter, as were many of their festivals, Stenia and Thesmophoria (Gilhus, 29–35).

There are even several examples of mirth in Homer's epic *Iliad* (Pope, trans. 1899, 32), including this bit where the gods are cooling their jets over some Ambrosia Lite, doing a little karaoke, and generally chillin':

Vulcan with awkward grace his office plies,
And unextinguish'd laughter shakes the skies.

It's the same in Rome. Many of the major Roman festivals, writes H. H. Scullard (1981), are thinly disguised excuses for drinking, laughter, and riotous behavior. A survey of just the major spring festivals bears this out. The *Compitalia*, generally held from January 3–5, featured "jollity, dancing and games" (59); *Faunus*, on February 13, was a "wild spirit of the countryside" and was celebrated with "dancing and merry-making" (72); Lupercalia, two days later, on February 15, included mostly naked young men running around smacking people with bloody strips of goat flesh, "rowdy" feasting, mayhem, and general laughter (77); *Matronalia*, on March 1, was a festival of Mars dominated by dancing, gifts, and "a general feeling of jollity" (87); and *Parilia*, on April 21, must have been quite a day with people drinking hot wine, jumping over burning bales of hay, and enjoying "a general festive mood" where the "drunken crowd" celebrated "merry-making" long into the night with "public rejoicing." April 21 was also the anniversary of the founding of Rome (105).

It's in this context that David Garland places the advice on laughter in Ephesians 5:4, "Entirely out of place is obscene, silly, and vulgar talk; but instead, let there be thanksgiving." Garland equates the laughter of Martial, Juvenal, Palutus, and various festivals with the coarse, risqué sexual humor specifically decried in the verse, not the kind of spontaneous, joyful humor mentioned elsewhere. The writer of Ephesians is not warning the reader against *all* humor and laughter, just this kind (2007, pers. comm.).

The often-funny Roman poet Horace (Ferry, trans. 2001, 33) also weighed in on the subject, writing with humor and wit on a variety of topics, both mundane and profound, and was widely celebrated at the time for doing so:

If, as Mimnermus says, there's no fun in living
If living's no fun, then let's have fun, why not?

Here Beginneth the Digression

There is ample evidence that the Romans had a wacky sense of humor. The ancient fertility festival of Floria, held on April 27, was claimed by the prostitutes of Rome as their own, and they performed plays in the nude and even fought gladiator-styled contests in the buff. At night, it was traditional for the city to be extravagantly lit with torches. During the reign of the powerful, mercurial—and bald—Emperor Tiberius, the praetor Lucius Apronius Caesianus once hired five thousand boys with shaven heads to light the way for the emperor and the crowd returning from a late-night theatrical production.

Generally, stories like this end with the emperor gaily hanging what's left of Caesianus from the gibbet while the audience laughs and applauds his wit. However, Tiberius evidently did have a sense of humor—and so Caesianus got away with his dangerous jibe.

Still, Tiberius decreed that from that time forward, all bald persons would be called *Caesiani* (Scullard 1981, 111).

Here Endeth the Digression

Perhaps some of Paul's obvious distaste for humor and laughter (as seen in the previous chapter) arose from the fact that, in the Roman Empire at least, a great deal of the state entertainment had become inextricably interwoven with pagan religions and holidays, where ribald humor and laughter were part and parcel of the show (Gilhus 1997, 58–59). Gilhus also observes that many of the noted Roman writers of the early Christian era savagely parodied and attacked Christianity, using bitter humor and satire, laced with derisive laughter (55–59). Paul's response, then, is only natural.

Early (and Not-So-Early) Church Fathers

Where it all really went south was when the guys *after* the New Testament, backed by the pervasive and merciless power of the CHURCH, started making pronouncements about what the people who wrote the Bible *really* meant. Many of the most influential early church leaders wrote during the so-called Dark Ages after the fall of Rome. (It seems to me that their often brutal, uncompromising, damnation-dominated theology is what that *made* those dismal times so dark for the common folk, who were already spending most of their energy trying to avoid various plagues, droughts, Goths, Visigoths, Vikings, Vandals, tax collectors, and famines!)

But as we shall see, the unquenchable joy that bubbles up in the human spirit wasn't totally eradicated during these grim days, despite the best efforts of St. John Chrysostom, St. Augustine, and Tertullian.

One of the foremost purveyors of this dark judgment and sinful death-oriented version of Christianity was a fourth-century Greek theologian and church leader, John Chrysostom, whose name (ironically) means "golden-mouthed." It is St. John C. who had the most to say on the topics of laughter and a lighthearted spirit:

> *Blessed are they that mourn, and woe unto them that laugh*, saith Christ [Matt 5:4]. How then saith Paul, *Rejoice in the Lord always* [Luke 6:25]? Is he not here opposed to Christ? God forbid. Woe to them that laugh, said Christ, hinting at the laughter of this world, which ariseth from the things which are present. (1843, 157; emphasis is not mine this time)

Dost thou wish to be far removed from foul words? Avoid not only foul words, but also inordinate laughter, and every kind of lust. (Schaff 1956, 9:443)

Suppose some persons laugh. Do thou on the other hand weep for their transgression! Many also once laughed at Noah whilst he was preparing the ark; but when the flood came, he laughed at them; or rather, the just man never laughed at them at all, but wept and bewailed! When therefore thou seest persons laughing, reflect that those teeth, that grin now, will one day have to sustain that most dreadful wailing and gnashing, and that they will remember this same laugh on That Day whilst they are grinding and gnashing! Then thou too shalt remember this laugh! How did the rich man laugh at Lazarus! But afterwards, when he beheld him in Abraham's bosom, he had nothing left to do but to bewail himself! (Schaff 1956, 9:481)

St. John C. doesn't sound like he's exactly overflowing with the milk of human kindness. And he's not done yet:

And thou standest laughing, raising a laugh after the manner of women of the world who are on stage. This has overthrown, this has cast down everything. Our affairs, both our business and our politeness, are turned into laughing; there is nothing steady, nothing grave. I say not these things to men of the world only; but I know those whom I am hinting at. For the Church has been filled with laughter. Whatever clever thing one may say, immediately there is laughter among those present: and the marvelous thing is that many do not leave off laughing even during the time of the prayer.

Everywhere the devil leads the dance, he has entered into all, is master of all. Christ is dishonored, is thrust aside; the Church is made no account of. Do ye not hear Paul saying, Let "filthiness and foolish talking and jesting" (Eph. v. 4) be put away from you? He places "jesting" along with "filthiness," and dost thou laugh? What is "foolish talking"? that which has nothing profitable. And dost thou, a solitary, laugh at all and relax thy countenance? Thou that art crucified? Thou that art a mourner? Tell me, doest thou laugh? **Where dost thou hear of Christ doing this? Nowhere; but that He was sad indeed oftentimes.** (Schaff 1956, 14:441–2, emphasis mine this time)

The most often-quoted passage is where Chrysostom states that Jesus never laughed. This offhand remark would, alas, become hugely influential and repeated *ad nauseum* for centuries to come.

But St. John C. was not the only powerful voice against humor or gaiety, wherever it might be found during those dismal days. Tertullian, who predates Chrysostom, is reported to have said that "nothing is more due to vanity than laughter" (Tertullian 1941, 471) and thundered that "vile jocularity" would be severely judged by a wrathful God (Tertullian 1959, 88). And then there is dour, doleful, hagridden St. Augustine who, in some religious circles, still exercises as much authority today as St. Paul. Augustine of Hippo, a contemporary of St. John C., had plenty to say about the subject of laughter and humor in his voluminous writings:

> Why then was my delight of such sort that I did it not alone? Because none doth ordinarily laugh alone? Ordinarily no one; yet laughter sometimes masters men alone and singly when no one whatever is with them, if anything very ludicrous presents itself to their senses or mind. (Pusey 1909, 31)

—ɯ—

> Yea, and so was he then beyond me: for he verily was the happier; not only for that he was thoroughly drenched in mirth, I disembowelled with cares: but he, by fair wishes, had gotten wine; I, by lying, was seeking for empty, swelling praise. (90)

Here Beginneth the Digression

There is a curious correlation at work here. At least during this era, the guys who had the most to say against laughter and humor are often the guys most likely to be anti-woman, too. Marina Warner notes that St. Augustine blamed women almost exclusively for the Fall and everything bad that's ever happened since. St. John Chrysostom was particularly graphic in his disgust of womankind:

> The whole of her bodily beauty is nothing less than phlegm, blood, bile, rheum, and the fluid of digested food . . . If you consider what is stored up behind those lovely eyes, the angle of the nose, the mouth and the cheeks, you will agree that the well-proportioned body is merely a whitened sepulcher. (Warner 1976, 58)

While Tertullian wondered aloud why all women just didn't kill themselves in shame:

> The sentence of God on this sex of yours lives on even in our times and so it is necessary that the guilt should live on, also. You are the one who opened the door to the Devil, you are the one who first plucked the fruit of the forbidden tree, you are the first who deserted the divine law; you are the one who persuaded him whom the Devil was not strong enough to attack. All too easily you destroyed the image of God, man. Because of your desert, that is, death, even the Son of God had to die! (Tertullian 1959, 118)

On the other hand, St. Augustine, the most influential proponent of the concept of "Original Sin"—which is behind much of the anti-woman, anti-comic pronouncements of the Dark Ages—really liked his mom and thought she was something of an exception despite being a woman and all.

Here Endeth the Digression

St. Jerome has serious injunctions against laughter (he particularly railed against "guffawing"—*cachinni*) in his various writings (Adkin 1985, 6:149–150). Other influential (and always stern) admonishments against laughter, humor, mirth, even smiling can be found in the works of Pope Gregory the Great, Basil, St. Ambrose, Benedict of Aniane, Isidore of Seville, and St. Columban (who ordered "six strokes" for giggling while singing), as well as the lives of a handful of saints who were notable mainly for never smiling or laughing during their lives, including Eugendus, St. Anthony, and St. Martin of Tours (Resnick 1987, 97:90–100).

Divine Comedy?

Even Dante, whose *Divine Comedy* marks the greatest joke of all, wasn't real big on normal people laughing much, as these lines from the "Paradise" cantos show (Alighieri in Longfellow trans. 1893, 588):

> Christ did not to his first disciples say,
>> "Go forth, and to the world preach idle tales,"
>> But unto them a true foundation gave;

And this so loudly sounded from their lips,
    That, in the warfare to enkindle Faith,
    They made of the Evangel shields and lances.

Now men go forth with jests and drolleries
    To preach, and if but well the people laugh,
    The hood puffs out, and nothing more is asked.

Monastic Communities

Monastic communities were especially austere. One of the most famous admonitions comes from the Egyptian monastic order, where the Pachomian monk Ammonius (now there's an unfortunate choice of names) demanded that monks never laugh and ordered particularly severe penalties for laughter at mealtimes. In a similar vein, the Syrian, Ephraem wrote:

> Laughter is the beginning of the destruction of soul; o monk, when you notice something of that, know that you have arrived at the depth of the evil. Then do not cease to pray God, that he might rescue from this death . . . Laughter expels the virtues and pushes aside the thoughts on death and meditation on the punishment. (Gilhus 1997, 65; citing Frank 1964, 145)

Still another well-loved, well-respected figure was the sixteenth-century Spaniard, St. Ignatius of Loyola, founder of the Jesuits, who provided a series of "exercises" for Christians, two of which directly involve the topic of joy and laughter:

> The sixth: not to wish to think of pleasing or joyful matters, as of glory, resurrection, etc., because any consideration of joy and gladness hinders us from feeling pain, sorrow and tears for our sins; but to keep before me that I wish to sorrow and feel pain, bringing rather to memory death, the judgment.

—ɯ—

> The eighth: not to laugh, nor to say what moves to laughter. (Lattey 1928, 37–38)

This is the same fellow who recommends pain as a means of penance, but says that that pain should be "sensible"—and that "it should not penetrate to the bones, so that it may cause pain and not illness" (39). And for that concession, at least, I suppose we should be grateful to St. Ignatius.

The screenplay adaptation of Umberto Eco's novel *The Name of the Rose* (1983) expresses the dichotomy of laughter as sin better than I could. It's a tense encounter between William of Baskerville (played in the movie by Sean Connery) and Jorge of Burgos (played by Feodor Chaliapin Jr.) in the library of a doomed and perverse monastery, where murders are occurring at an alarming rate. Jorge of Burgos has just attacked Baskerville (a nod to Sherlock Holmes) because he's heard laughter in the room where the monks are (usually) silently copying manuscripts:

Jorge:	You, Franciscans, however, belong to an Order where merriment is viewed with indulgence.
William:	Yes, it's true. Saint Francis was much disposed to laughter.
Jorge:	Laughter is a devilish wind which deforms the lineaments of the face and makes men look like monkeys.
William:	Monkeys do not laugh. Laughter is particular to man . . .
Jorge:	. . . as a sin. Christ never laughed.
William:	Can we be so sure?
Jorge:	There is nothing in the Scriptures to say that He did.
William:	And there's nothing there to say that He did not. (pause) Even the saints have been known to employ comedy . . .
Jorge:	. . . to ridicule the enemies of the faith.
William:	For example, when the pagans plunged Saint Maurus into the boiling water, he complained that his bath was cold. The Sultan put his hand in—and scalded himself.
Jorge:	A saint immersed in boiling water does not play childish tricks. He restrains his cries and suffers for the truth.
William:	And yet, Aristotle devoted his second book of poetics to comedy as an instrument of truth.
Jorge:	You have read this work?
William:	No, of course not. It's been lost for many centuries.
Jorge:	No, it is not! It was never written! Because Providence doesn't want futile things glorified.
William:	Oh, that I must contest . . .
Jorge:	Enough! This abbey is overshadowed by grief. Yet you would intrude on our sorrow with idle banter!
William:	Forgive me, Venerable Jorge. My remarks were truly out of place.

On the Other Hand . . .

Even as the rules against virtually everything, save for piety, prayer, and penance tightened in the medieval monasteries, and as the church fathers became more and more convinced that laughter threatened the church's hold on her people, there were still those who bravely disagreed. The comic spirit, like the human spirit, can hardly be tamped down indefinitely.

Saint Francis of Assisi

The best-loved, best-known proponent of a joyous lifestyle was St. Francis of Assisi, the world's first hippie, founder of the Franciscans (as noted by Brother William above), and an extraordinarily radical young man, particularly for that day and time. He called his followers the *Jongleurs de Dieu* (roughly, "Tumblers of Our Lord"), and in that name, writes G.K. Chesterton, is one of the keys to understanding his transformation:

> St. Francis really meant what he said when he said he had found the secret of life in being the servant and the secondary figure. There was to be found ultimately in such service a freedom almost amounting to frivolity. It was comparable to the condition of the jongleur because it almost amounted to frivolity. The jester could be free when the knight was rigid; and it was possible to be a jester in the service which is perfect freedom. (Chesterton 2001, 78)

Just as there is no limit to what can get done in a community when nobody cares who gets the credit, there is no limit to the joy you can spread if you are totally without ego, totally without self. If, like the tumbler or jester, you'll do or say anything without regard to making yourself look good or justified, then there is no limit to the happiness you can spread. The definitive three-volume life and works of St. Francis lists literally hundreds of quotes attributed to Francis related to happiness and joy (Armstrong, Hellmann, Short 1999, 59, 71).

St. Francis wasn't the only saint to expound on mirth and a joyful heart. St. Philip Neri, sometimes called "the good Pippo" was a sixteenth-century native of Florence and founder of the influential religious group, the Congregation of the Oratory. St. Neri was widely celebrated for his joyful humor and predilection for jokes, japes, and eloquent puncturings of the pompous. Pope Gregory XIV even tried to make him a cardinal, but St. Neri declined; he much preferred to dance and sing gaily in front of the church establishment whenever he could (Laude 2005, 164–5).

The Feast of Fools

But here's the wonderful, crazy thing. Even as the hierarchy of the Roman Church and the most influential of the church fathers continued to insist that a sober, penitent, low-grade misery for mankind's (and especially womankind's) degraded, fallen state was the *only* appropriate response to life in and out of the church, *the desperate need for joy and happiness and laughter would not be denied.* The Feast of Fools was an extraordinary medieval religious festival celebrated in parts of Europe, usually (though not always) before or on January 1. There were several variations, under different names, but all had one element in common. During the Feast of Fools, all roles reversed—priests wore strangely sexual masks and behaved in a suggestive or loony fashion, townspeople became priests; everybody sang outrageous songs, parodied high church leaders, and verbally attacked the pompous and the proud. In some towns, the people even elected a "Boy Bishop" to preside. Everything was upside-down.

The Council of Basel finally banned the Feast of Fools in 1431, though it survived in different forms well into the 1500s. We can still see remnants of it today in the nearly universal revelry that accompanies New Year's Eve. But in medieval times, on this one occasion, everybody was allowed to blow off steam in the most repressive of societies, where the church invaded every part of every life, dictating what you ate, thought, did, or said (Cox 1969, 3–7).

According to Harvey Cox, the Feast of Fools was important, perhaps essential. Long after its official demise, the Feast was covertly sanctioned and supported by the church as a necessary outlet in a hardscrabble life. The implications for today are obvious:

> Laughter is hope's last weapon. Crowded on all sides with idiocy and ugliness, pushed to concede that the final apocalypse seems to be upon us, we seem nonetheless to nourish laughter as our only remaining defense. Or perhaps better stated, our laughter is our way of crossing ourselves. It shows that despite the disappearance of any empirical basis for hope, we have not stopped hoping. (157)

In the spirit of the Feast of Fools, just like the spirit of Christmas shorn of all of its commercial trappings, Cox sees something universal:

> This gift of comic hope is not something on which religious people hold a monopoly. They share it with all sorts and conditions of men. But it may be the special responsibility of men of faith to nourish this gift, to celebrate this sense of comic hope, and to demonstrate it. It could conceivably disappear, and where laughter and hope have disappeared man has ceased to be man. (157)

The Feast of Fools may have contained the tribal memory of the ancient Roman festival of Saturnalia, where masters waited on their servants and a mock king—*Saturnalia princeps*—was elected (Scullard 1981, 206–207).

Did You Hear the One about the Reformation?

Still, the power of the church was such that this obsession with maintaining a doleful, grieving gravity, or something like that, as a condition of salvation was (mostly) continued for hundreds of years. Fortunately, you can't blame Martin Luther for this point of view's continuance. Luther, in the first half of the sixteenth century, was something of a medieval John Belushi, according to numerous accounts. One of the numerous examples of Luther's wit is his response to the claim that he was the catalyst for the Reformation:

> I simply taught, preached and wrote God's word; otherwise I did nothing. And while I slept or drank Wittenberg beer with my friends Philip and Amsdorf, the Word so greatly weakened the papacy that no prince or emperor ever inflicted such losses upon it. (Todd 1982, 238)

Some of his funniest routines can't be repeated here, but this was a guy who was long alleged to have had the Lord's Prayer inscribed at the bottom of his favorite beer stein and then raced his friends to drain their goblets to see who could recite it first. This apparently got more difficult as the evening wore on (*The Wittenburg Door* 2005).

But, as Jürgen Moltmann reminds us, while the Reformation worked to help end penances and indulgences, its leaders also abolished holidays and games:

> This led to the establishment of the Puritan society of penny pinchers and to the industrial workaday world among the very people who had at first insisted on believing that men are justified by faith alone. (Moltmann 1972, 11)

(By the way, John Knox's venomous *The First Blast of the Trumpet against the Monstrous Regiment of Women,* published not long thereafter in 1558, isn't all that wild about laughter and humor, either. I sense a trend here . . .)

In 1599, both the Archbishop of Canterbury and the Bishop of London prohibited the publication of satire and ordered that works by Ben Jonson, Joseph Hall, John Marston, Thomas Nashe, and others be incinerated. Jonson and Marston later invented "comic satire" to get around the ban (Elliott 1965, 331–32).

Luther was unique in a lot of ways. More typical of the official church response to joyfulness are the writings of Thomas Hobbes. In the years following its publication in 1651, Hobbes' *Leviathan* was required reading. Here's a sample of his thoughts on the subject:

> *Sudden Glory*, is the passion which maketh those *Grimaces* called LAUGHTER; and is caused either by some sudden act of their own, that pleaseth them; or by the apprehension of some deformed thing in another, by comparison whereof they suddenly applaud themselves. And it is incident most to them, that are conscious of the fewest abilities in themselves; who are forced to keep themselves in their own favour, by observing the imperfections of other men. And therefore much Laughter at the defects of others, is a signe of Pusillanimity. For of great minds, one of the proper workes is, to help and free others from scorn; and compare themselves onely with the most able. (Hobbes 1931, 27; emphasis is original this time)

Hobbes obviously doesn't think much of laughter *or* people who laugh. Still, he includes this curious sentence a few lines later, which would almost make the modern reader think that Tom at least knew a good joke when he heard one, whether he would publicly admit it or not: "For no man Laughs at old jests; or Weeps for an old calamity" (27).

Blame It on the Puritans

For most of the last several hundred years, *Leviathan* has typified the attitude of both the Roman Catholic Church and the majority of the Protestant faiths towards humor. But not since the days of Irish monks shivering in their cells working on the *Book of Kells* had anybody taken this dour, unceasingly depressive outlook as seriously as the Puritans. Nobody took more pleasure in *not* taking pleasure. The most famous sustained attack on humor and laughter comes from the Puritan document, *Histrio-Mastix*, primarily by William Prynne. This incredibly grim 1,150-page manifesto against the theater also devotes several hundred pages to railing against humor. Pascal Covici's summary includes this torturous bit of prose from the book:

(T)he laughter Playes occasion, (which is their chiefest end,) is a suffi-
cient evidence of their excessive folly; and so is ground enough for
Christians, for all men to condemne them as vanities, as fooleries, as
Clements Alexandrinus, and other Fathers doe at large declare.
   Stage-laughter . . . is altogether unseemly, unseasonable unto
Christians . . . (because) altogether inconsistent with the gravity,
modesty, and sobriety of a Christian, whose affectations should be
more sublime, more serious and composed, then to be immoderately
tickled with meere lascivious vanities, or to lash out in excessive
cachinnations in the publike view of dissolute graceless persons, who
will be hardened and encouraged in their lascivious courses, by their
ill example. (1997, 213)

Prynne later maintains that Jesus "was always mourning, never
laughing," and that "Paul likewise wept night and day for yeeres
together, but that he never laughed, neither doth he himselfe shew any
where nor any other for him" (Covici, 213).

Finally, Covici flatly notes, that despite some individual diary entries
from well-known Puritans John Winthrop and Nathaniel Ward to the
contrary, "that Puritans and their descendants in the main distrusted
humor seems true beyond any cavil" (210).

Even more famous through extensive reprinting, particularly in the
United States (perhaps because no one really wanted to wade through
all 1,150 pages of *Histrio-Mastix*), is Robert Barclay's widely dissemi-
nated *An Apology for the True Christian Divinity* from 1678:

That it is not lawful to use games, sports, plays, nor among other
things, comedies among Christians, under the notion of recreations,
which do not agree with Christian silence, gravity, and sobriety: for
laughing, sporting, gaming, mocking, jesting, vain talking, &c., is not
Christian liberty, nor harmless mirth. (870)

In many places, the admonishments of Prynne and Barclay were
broadly accepted as carrying the same weight as Scripture itself. The influential eighteenth-century English nobleman and author, Philip Dormer
Stanhope, the Fourth Earl of Chesterfield, was also highly emulated in his
day. His letters to his son (actually thinly disguised sermons on morality)
were widely read and admired by people aspiring to a lofty social status:

Loud laughter is the mirth of the mob, who are only pleased with silly
things; for true wit or good sense never excited a laugh since the cre-

ation of the world. A man of parts and fashion is therefore only seen to smile, but never heard to laugh. (1847, 211)

—⁂—

Loud laughter is extremely inconsistent with *les bienséances*, as it is only the illiberal and noisy testimony of the joy of the mob at some very silly thing. A gentleman is often seen, but very seldom heard to laugh. (164)

Here Beginneth the Digression

The full title of Prynne's book is a thigh-slapper itself:

Histrio-Mastix. The players scourge, or, actors tragædie, divided into two parts. Wherein it is largely evidenced, by divers arguments, by the concurring authorities and resolutions of sundry texts of Scripture, That popular stage-plays are sinfull, heathenish, lewde, ungodly spectacles, and most pernicious corruptions; condemned in all ages, as intolerable mischiefes to churches, to republickes, to the manners, mindes, and soules of men. And that the profession of play-poets, of stage-players; together with the penning, acting, and frequenting of stage-playes, are unlawfull, infamous and misbeseeming Christians. All pretences to the contrary are here likewise fully answered; and the unlawfulnes of acting, of beholding academicall enterludes, briefly discussed; besides sundry other particulars concerning dancing, dicing, health-drinking, &c. of which the table will informe you.

It was published in London in 1633, which—unfortunately for Prynne—was the year Queen Henrietta Maria and her ladies performed in a play for the court. The Court of Star Chamber, England's notorious kangaroo "court," promptly (and roughly) cut off Prynne's ears (Covici 1997, 211–12). For extra measure, they fined him 5,000 pounds, imprisoned him for life, burned "S.L." into his cheeks (for "seditious libeler"), and yanked his degree from Oxford, which probably was the unkindest cut of all.

Here Endeth the Digression

But perhaps the best known proponent of this philosophy was the legendary preacher, Jonathan Edwards. In 1733, he delivered a fiery sermon titled "Sinners in the Hands of an Angry God" that was destined to be repeated—in various forms—for decades to come. Few better examples of the (in)famous "Hellfire and Brimstone" sermon exist:

> They are now the objects of that very same anger and wrath of God, that is expressed in the torments of Hell. And the reason why they do not go down to Hell at each moment, is not because God, in whose power they are, is not then very angry with them; as he is with many miserable creatures now tormented in Hell, who there feel and bear the fierceness of his wrath. Yea, God is a great deal more angry with great numbers that are now on earth: yea, doubtless, with many that are now in this congregation, who it may be are at ease, than he is with many of those who are now in the flames of Hell.
>
> So that it is not because God is unmindful of their wickedness, and does not resent it, that he does not let loose his hand and cut them off. God is not altogether such a one as themselves, though they may imagine him to be so. The wrath of God burns against them, their damnation does not slumber; the pit is prepared, the fire is made ready, the furnace is now hot, ready to receive them; the flames do now rage and glow. The glittering sword is whet, and held over them, and the pit hath opened its mouth under them. (Edwards 2005, 401–402)

There was not much room for happy laughter and fun in Edwards' theology!

And so it continued. The fact that each new generation of preacher and priest felt compelled to orate against humor, however, implies to me that laughter never quite went away in the church or elsewhere. Not surprisingly, Edwards' words were echoed a century later by still *another* writer and pastor, John Angell James, who believed that each snicker or chortle opened the door to allow Satan into your life:

> It is hard to conceive how earnestness and spirituality can be maintained by those whose tables are covered, and whose leisure time is consumed, by the bewitching inspirations of the god of laughter. There is little hope of our arresting the evil, except we make it our great business to raise up a ministry who shall not themselves be carried away with the torrent; who shall be grave, without being gloomy; serious, without being melancholy; and who, on the other hand, shall be cheerful without being frivolous, and whose chastened mirthfulness shall check, or at any rate reprove, the excesses of their companions.

> Nothing can be more opposed to the serious spirit which true religion requires, or more destructive of it, than this constant supply of new materials for laughter. Nor does the mischief stop with the young and the worldly, it is infecting the professors of religion. (James 1847, 198–99)

Like St. John Chrysostom, Barclay, and Edwards before him, James felt personally affronted by those who dared to laugh. It is the most extreme manifestation of Puritanism, and a worldview that would dominate American spiritual and secular life, deep into the twentieth century.

Whatever we believe about the sinfulness of spontaneous laughter now, James' observations reflected the norm in much of the Western world during his day. Charles Baudelaire, the influential French wit of the nineteenth century, observed how the Christians he knew almost feared to laugh:

> [T]he Sage *par excellence*, the Word Incarnate, never laughed. In the eyes of One who has all knowledge and all power, the comic does not exist. And yet the Word Incarnate knew anger; He even knew tears. (Baudelaire 1965, 450)

Later, Baudelaire sadly noted that, for most devout Christians of his era, "Holy Books never laugh, to whatever nations they may belong . . ." (Baudelaire, 455).

Increase Mather, recently the subject of a fine biography, *The Last American Puritan* (Hall 1988), was certainly one of the most influential Puritans of his day (the late 1600s). So much so, he vowed never to smile in public (353). This preacher, author, and president of Harvard worked tirelessly to end anything not related to church or work. He created laws that would whip parents for not bringing their kids to church, enacted punishment against those who swore and those who heard the swearing but didn't report it, created a network of citizen-spies to report alcohol consumption. He even created the "Provoking Evils" laws that penalized leisure activities, including "sociability and idle talk": All that was flirtatious, merry, jocose, or high-spirited Mather condemned because it disguised human corruption and diverted attention from God's righteousness (108–109).

Exactly how much the Puritans are to blame—or, depending on your point of view, how much *credit* is due to the Puritans—is hard to gauge.

Influential writer and critic H. L. Mencken flatly blamed the Puritans and their successors for America's (and, by extension, the American churches') aversion to laughter. The last chapter of his book *A Book of Prefaces* (1927) fingers the Puritans for a lot of things that he believed were wrong in America. He includes the Puritans' impact on literature and their unrelenting assault on humor and laughter. Among Mencken's observations:

> The Puritan's utter lack of aesthetic sense, his distrust of all romantic emotions, his unmatchable intolerance of opposition, his unbreakable belief in his own bleak and narrow views, his savage cruelty of attack, his lust for relentless and barbarous persecution—these things have put an almost unbreakable burden upon the exchange of ideas in the United States, and particularly upon that form of it which involves playing with them for the mere game's sake. (201–202)
>
> Philistinism is no more than another name for Puritanism. Both wage a ceaseless warfare upon beauty in its every form, from painting to religious ritual, and from the drama to the dance—the first because it holds beauty to be a mean and stupid thing, and the second because it holds beauty to be distracting and corrupting. (203)
>
> The American is school-mastered out of gusto, out of joy, out of innocence. He can never fathom William Blake's notion that "the lust of the goat is also to the glory of God." He must be correct, or, in his own phrase, he must bust. (281–82)

And it was Mencken who once famously wrote, "Puritanism—The haunting fear that someone, somewhere, may be happy" (1949, 624). Certainly some of the most famous books about Puritans—*The Scarlet Letter* and *The Crucible*—and their own writings (most notably *Sinners in the Hands of an Angry God*) tend to reinforce that perception.

Still, there is some evidence that the image of the unrelentingly angry, joyless Puritan may not be *completely* accurate. Michael Kammen's influential *Mystic Chords of Memory* (1993) unflinchingly examines how America acquired a past it really didn't have, and how our collective memories and apparent history have been distorted and manufactured for various political and religious agendas. Chapter 7 of his book explores the idea that, "Memory is what we now have in place of religion" (194–227).

Kammen then systematically dissects what the Puritans actually were and what they eventually came to symbolize in American religious and civic life. For much of American history, what were generally believed to be Puritan ideals were considered admirable (or particularly "American") and worthy of emulation. However, Puritans eventually came to be universally condemned as narrow-minded, dour, intolerant, self-righteous, and humorless. And, as Kammen notes, there was certainly some grounds for those charges. These were the people, after all, who banned Christmas!

But he claims that, to a significant degree, the ghastly, ghostly Calvinism of the Puritans is, in large part, shaped by the anti-Puritan writings and allusions of a number of influential politicians and New York-based writers with particular axes to grind. Kammen writes, "That Puritan-bashing became trendy during the 1920s is well established and well documented" (388).

Whether or not it was *wholly* deserved, the damage was done. The widely admired but (apparently) dour, humorless Puritan had been the norm for more than two hundred years of American life. Accurate or not, that was the model most American churches emulated. It wasn't until midway into the twentieth century that anyone began to question the veracity of that picture.

CHAPTER 5

"The redeemed ought to look more like it!"

The sense of humour is, in many respects, a more adequate resource for the incongruities of life than the spirit of philosophy. If we are able to laugh at the curious quirks of fortune in which the system of order and meaning which each life constructs within and around itself is invaded, we at least do not make the mistake of prematurely reducing the irrational to a nice system. —Reinhold Niebuhr (1946)

In time, things change.

In time, church-people eventually discovered—and if they didn't embrace, they at least learned to tolerate—the presence of humor, unfettered happiness, and occasionally outright hilarity. Not necessarily *in* church, but at least in the parking lot (or, in certain *really* radical congregations in the 1960s and 70s, in the narthex, where newcomer and old-timer alike jockeyed for position by the pre-service, pre-Starbucks coffee and Danish).

What happened? Humor, of course, never went away in the non-church world. It's just that eventually in most Western nations the non-church world became bigger than the church world in the daily lives of people. Mark Twain, Oscar Wilde, Charlie Chaplin, Buster Keaton, the Marx Brothers, and a host of others happened. They employed humor, sometimes as a tool, sometimes as a hammer, sometimes as a crutch, and sometimes just for the sheer exhilaration of it. The humor of the world ranged from witty wordplay to gleefully chaotic slapstick tinged with anarchy. And gradually, many believers gratefully surrendered to it.

In the face of that onslaught, the church gave ground grudgingly. All along, the issue of the church's dominance had been about power. Anything that challenged the church's power was anathema. And humor—riotous, uncontrollable, milk-out-of-your-nose laughter—is simply *not* controllable. As anybody who has gotten a case of the giggles during a church service or—heavens!—a funeral can attest. One of the great *Mary Tyler Moore Show* episodes involves Mary helplessly giggling and snorting at the funeral service of Chuckles the Clown (dressed as Peter Peanut, Chuckles was killed when an elephant sat on him).

You control humor the same way you control anything in the religious world—you declare it a sin (maybe even a mortal sin) or call it heresy. As one Christian writer who could be very, very funny when he wanted to, G. K. Chesterton, put it, "Every heresy has been an effort to narrow the Church" (2001, 179). But by the mid-to-late-1880s, the cat was irretrievably out of the bag. Even if the church itself was still resistant, Christians were not.

The Storytellers

A group of English authors were among the first to regularly write with humor from a Christian worldview. Like Chesterton, George Macdonald wrote in a dazzling variety of genres. While some of his work remains compelling today (*On the Back of the North Wind, The Princess and the Goblin*), other books have slowly fallen from favor, their writing too dense, too descriptive, too much a product of their time for modern readers. Still, Macdonald had much to say on the topic of faith and mirth:

> I wonder how many Christians there are who so thoroughly believe God made them that they can laugh in God's name; who understand that God invented laughter and gave it to His children. Such belief would add a keenness to the zest in their enjoyment, and slay that feeble laughter in which neither heart nor intellect has a share.
>
> It would help them also to understand the depth of this miracle. The Lord of gladness delights in the laughter of a merry heart. (1871, 23)

Macdonald's admirers included a group of English writers who met regularly at The Eagle and Child pub in Oxford, most notably J. R. R. Tolkien and C. S. Lewis. Both were Christians who wrote stories that are among the most beloved books in the English language. While there is humor in Tolkien's monumental *The Lord of the Rings* trilogy, it is mostly incidental to the thundering sweep of empires and war. *The Hobbit* and other, smaller, books such as *Leaf by Niggle* are more overtly lighthearted.

Tolkien didn't have much to say about humor in the church, but Lewis was positively prolific on the topic, even in the Narnia series of children's stories. In *The Magician's Nephew*, the great lion Aslan has just spoken the universe into existence. He's creating all of the creatures, both Dumb Beasts and Talking Beasts. After the Jackdaw makes an embarrassing *faux pas,* the talking animals try unsuccessfully to repress their laughter. But Aslan says it is okay, guffaw away:

> "Laugh and fear not, creatures. Now that you are no longer dumb and witless, you need not always be grave. For jokes as well as justice come in with speech."
>
> So they all let themselves go. And there was such merriment that the Jackdaw himself plucked up courage again and perched on the cab-horse's head, between its ears, clapping its wings, and said:
>
> "Aslan! Aslan! Have I made the first joke? Will everybody always be told how I made the first joke?"
>
> "No, little friend," said the Lion. "You have not made the first joke; you have only been the first joke." Then everyone laughed more than ever; but the Jackdaw didn't mind and laughed just as loud till the horse shook its head and the Jackdaw lost its balance and fell off, but remembered its wings (they were still new to it) before it reached the ground. (Lewis 1955, 143)

Lewis' great comic novel, *The Screwtape Letters,* is profoundly funny—literally! Reversing the natural order of the universe (one of the core concepts of satire) allowed Lewis to make some heavy-duty observations about the nature of Christians and Christianity in the twentieth century. But adopting the mind-set of a couple of demons to make a spiritual point in a funny way had its emotional costs, alas, as Lewis wrote in his forward to a later addition to the canon, "Screwtape Proposes a Toast" (Lewis 2001, 183). An example of Lewis' droll humor appears near the end of the book, where Screwtape's demonic but dim nephew has committed a fatal blunder:

> "My dear, my very dear, Wormwood, my poppet, my pigsnie.
> "How mistakenly now that all is lost you come whimpering to ask me whether the terms of affection in which I address you meant nothing

from the beginning. Far from it! Rest assured, my love for you and your love for me are as like as two peas. The difference is that I am the stronger. I think they will give you to me now; or a bit of you. Love you? Why, yes. As dainty a morsel as ever I grew fat on." (Lewis 2001, 171)

In both Tsarist and Communist Russia, Christ-haunted writers also struggled with what to do about the intrusion of humor into the church, Christianity, and the lives of individual believers. One of the most magical such moments is in *The Brothers Karamazov* (1949). Fyodor Dostoevsky's dense, rich novel is, on the surface, about the apparent murder of a dissolute old man by one of his sons. But in fact, the book tackles nothing less than the cosmic struggle between faith and free will. In the midst of the sweeping, soaring language, conflict, and heavy doses of philosophy, Dostoevsky inserts this exquisite scene. The hero Alyosha is returning from another exhausting encounter with Rakitin and Grushenka and collapses in his cell, strangely jubilant. He dreams of the wedding in Cana and—mixed in with fragments of his encounters with his friends—sees the event in a new light. The purpose of Christ's first miracle, he discovers, is nothing else than to bring happiness and laughter to humanity:

> "Ah, yes, I was missing that, and I didn't want to miss it, I love that passage: it's Cana of Galilee, the first miracle.... Ah, that miracle! Ah, that sweet miracle! It was not men's grief, but their joy that Christ visited, He worked His first miracle to help men's gladness.... 'He who loves men loves their gladness, too' ... [The deceased] was always repeating that, it was one of his leading ideas ... 'There's no living without joy,' ... Mitya says.... Yes, Mitya.... 'Everything that is true and good is always full of forgiveness,' he used to say that, too." (277–78)

In time, other Christian writers would emerge, including Evelyn Waugh, Peter DeVries, Flannery O'Connor, Frederick Buechner, Walker Percy, Will Campbell, Wendell Berry, and even André Dubus III, all of whom have used humor in the course of their storytelling.

The Theologians

But for the great mass of Christians, laughter was something done everywhere *but* in the church. The persistent pressure and pervasive influence of the church fathers and the Puritans were simply too much to be overcome in just a few generations—and many church leaders liked it that way.

The secular world noticed, of course, including Frederich Nietzsche. Besides his oft-quoted statement, "The redeemed ought to look more like it!" Nietzsche once had his great creation Zarathustra lament:

> Verily, that Hebrew died too early whom the preachers of slow death honor; and for many it has become a calamity that he died too early. As yet he knew only tears and the melancholy of the Hebrew, and hatred of the good and the just—the Hebrew Jesus: then the longing for death overcame him. Would that he had remained in the wilderness and far from the good and the just! Perhaps he would have learned to live and to love the earth—and laughter, too. (Nietzsche 1956, 109)

There were plenty of Christians who still held on to the St. John Chrysostom/Puritan model. As late as 1959, the influential magazine, *The Christian Century*, published an article titled, "Humor: Plausible and

Demonic" (1959). The author William Hamilton railed against humor, saying it is on the side of "our conformist culture rather than against it" and that humor "can tell us what to be against; it cannot show us how to live." Hamilton wrote that humor impedes what should be our true goal, achieving a "purity of heart." But he didn't stop there. He noted that the "saddest cases" were contemporary writers who seek to "impose" a sense of humor on Jesus. Finally, he commended Reinhold Niebuhr's statement that there is [no] laughter in the holy of holies" (1946, 131). (More on this later.)

> My point is that we must now seek more passionately than ever to banish humor from the Holy of Holies. Our defenses of humor have been a pathetic attempt to keep in step with a secular culture that has nothing else. I am not calling for abolition of humor (though I would suggest that none of us ever again advise anyone to "cultivate a sense of humor"), but for its redemption. (Hamilton 1959, 807)

Somewhere, St. Augustine (but not Increase Mather) was smiling.

But Hamilton was swimming against the tide, at least as far as Christian writers (and readers) are concerned—although most churches still stand as bastions against laughter. Two figures in particular, Karl Barth and Elton Trueblood, led the final assault.

Karl Barth

Karl Barth (1886–1968) was a theological giant, one of the greats of the past hundred years. In an issue of *Theology Today* devoted solely to Barth, the lead editorial begins, "Any history of twentieth century theology will be largely the story of the revolutionary work and influence of Karl Barth" (Migliore 1986, 43:309). His thirteen-volume (and unfinished) *Church Dogmatics,* a "state of the nation" of theology, is one of the towering works of the last century. As Robert McAfee Brown notes, no work of modern theology can proceed without him. "One can responsibly disagree with Barth; one cannot responsibly ignore him" (1963, 2). No less an expert than Paul Tillich once wrote, in comparing Barth to Martin Luther, "Barth's greatness is that he corrects himself again and again in the light of the 'situation,' and that he strenuously tries not to become his own follower" (1951, 5).

Where Barth enters our discussion is that his major biographers report that he had a simply marvelous sense of humor, one that was well known throughout the theological community. Take, for instance, this quotation, where Barth pokes fun both at his own prolific output and at the tendency of so many scholars to turn into "Barthians":

> The angels laugh at old Karl. They laugh at him because he tries to grasp the truth about God in a book of *Dogmatics*. They laugh at the fact that volume follows volume and each is thicker than the previous one. As they laugh, they say to one another, "Look! Here he comes now with his little pushcart full of volumes of the *Dogmatics!*"
>
> And they laugh about the men who write so much about Karl Barth instead of writing about the things he is trying to write about. Truly, the angels laugh. (Brown 1963, 3)

Daniel L. Migliore fears that, for all of Barth's enduring impact, modern readers "miss something essential if they overlooked his remarkable freedom and playfulness." What makes Barth's humor more amazing is that in addition to his monumental theological writings, he courageously confronted Nazism and was a prophetic voice in ending Apartheid. And yet, "Laughter was deeply etched in Barth's theology and spirituality. He was a theologian with a rare sense of humor" (Migliore 1986, 43:311).

Perhaps Barth's humor stems from the fact that he really and truly *loved* his job:

> Theology . . . is a peculiarly beautiful science. Indeed, we can confidently say that it is the most beautiful of all sciences. To find the sciences distasteful is the mark of the Philistine. It is an extreme form of Philistinism to find, or to be able to find, theology distasteful. The theologian who has no joy in his work is not a theologian at all. Sulky faces, morose thoughts and boring ways of speaking are intolerable in this science. (Barth 1975, 656)

As the participants of the "Karl Barth Centennial Symposium" at Princeton Theological Seminary in 1986 stressed, they're not downplaying Barth's titanic contributions to theology—and, indeed, the church—by paying tribute to his lighthearted side. Instead, as Migliore suggests, one of Barth's "lasting contributions" to Christianity may have been his playful spirit and a sense of humor that was "born in the confidence of God's grace." For the little Swiss-born preacher, teacher, and theologian, this seems a fitting summation:

> His playful spirituality encourages us to look for the inbreaking of the Kingdom elsewhere than in the uptight and self-righteous ideologues of the right and the left who find it impossible to laugh at themselves and intolerable to be laughed at. (Migliore 1986, 43:314)

Barth gave generations of Christian writers, preachers, and thinkers permission to allow that "inbreaking of the Kingdom" to take place, even if it involved laughing from time to time.

D. Elton Trueblood

That all said, Barth—who wrote in German—was more of an influence on other theologians than he was on the pastors, priests, vestry, and deacons of the modern church. The writer who first reached that particular tier with the message that laughter and the church could coexist was D. Elton Trueblood (1900–1994), Quaker, educator, and author of *The Humor of Christ*, published in 1964. Trueblood (this is another one of those last names that seems perfectly designed to fit a specific profession—like Luke Skywalker) wrote nearly two dozen important, influential books. None, however, had the impact of *The Humor of Christ*.

Trueblood's journey with Jesus and mirth began while solemnly reading Matthew 7 to his four-year-old son. Suddenly, the little fellow breaks into gales of laughter:

> He laughed because he saw how preposterous it would be for a man to be so deeply concerned about a speck in another person's eye, that he was unconscious of the fact his own eye had a beam in it. Because the child understood perfectly that the human eye is not large enough to have a beam in it, the very idea struck him as ludicrous. His gay laughter was a rebuke to his parents for their failure to respond to humor in an unexpected place. (Trueblood 1964, 9)

Trueblood writes that it was then he began to consciously seek out examples of humor in Christ's life and teachings.

It probably should be admitted, however, that *The Humor of Christ* isn't exactly . . . well . . . *funny*. With a scholar's exactitude, Trueblood examines in detail all of Christ's prayers, parables, and pronouncements for *any* possibility of wry asides, subtle sarcasm, gentle smiling rebukes, and sly humor. For example, when talking about the need to witness to the good news in Mark 4:21, Jesus responds, "Is a lamp brought in to be put under a bushel, or under a bed, and not on a stand?" Trueblood gleefully notes:

> Since the lamp mentioned has an open flame and since the bed is a mattress, it is easy to see that in this situation the light would be suffocated or the mattress would be burned. The appeal here is to the patently absurd. The sensitive laugh, because they get the point. (18)

Well, maybe the word *laugh* overstates their probable response. At times, Trueblood seems to be reaching in his attempt to uncover the lighter side of faith, such as his blithe transitional statement, "Christ went with the gay crowd," that is, tax collectors and other sinners (20). (Still more proof, as if any were needed, that utilizing topical humor and current colloquialisms has always been risky business in writing!)

But Trueblood's impact is more cumulative than specific. Generations of thinkers and pastors have cited *The Humor of Christ* as the foundation of their efforts to create a more believable, more fully rounded image of Jesus of Nazareth. With Trueblood, the concept that Jesus may have laughed and that religion could encompass joy as well as anger and judgment gradually took hold in the second half of the twentieth century.

The Humorists

One piece of evidence for this growing acceptance was the surprise bestseller *The Gospel According to Peanuts* by Robert L. Short (1965). Short, then twenty-eight years old, was a young pastor who reluctantly transformed a slide show he'd been working on into a book length manuscript—only to see the book eventually sell 10 million copies and remain constantly in print (Short 1965, 4). If Trueblood spoke to pastors and seminarians, Short spoke—at last—to the laity.

The Gospel According to Peanuts, like *The Humor of Christ,* is rarely laugh-out-loud funny, but it is still a gentle treasure to read today, a series of sweet-spirited meditations on Charles M. Schulz's immortal characters, Charlie Brown, Lucy, Linus, and Snoopy (who gets his own chapter, "The Hound of Heaven"). Schulz was a Christian (he's quoted throughout the book), and, unlike many modern cartoonists, wrote and drew every panel of the cartoon throughout his long career.

One of the running gags in *Peanuts* was Charlie Brown's inability to fly a kite. After one such misadventure, Charlie Brown pounds the ground in frustration, "I'll *never* be able to get that kite in the air! *Never, never, never, never!*" In the very next panel, we see Snoopy lying comfortably on top of his doghouse, nonchalantly flying that same kite. After contrasting this scene with the final tragic scene of *King Lear*, as Lear helplessly cradles his murdered daughter, Short makes this observation:

> Christianity, like comedy, always involves a *genuine* fall, or reversal, that is nevertheless not *ultimately* serious. This is why the story of the creation, fall, and subsequent redemption of all men is finally a "divine comedy." (Short 1965, 120)

Like others before him, Short rejects the notion of "Christian tragedy" as a contradiction in terms. Instead, Christians—represented by Charlie Brown—need to take seriously the mercy of God, while training themselves not to take this present world seriously at all:

> Just as in all comedy there is a final redemption, Christianity contends there is a final redemption for all: "For as in Adam all die, so also in Christ shall all be made alive" (1 Cor 15:22). Therefore the laughter of comedy and the joy of Christ's gospel are *closely* related. (Short, 120)

By now, of course, other changes were afoot in society at large and in the church itself. The reforms of Vatican II (1962–65) and the sudden emergence of the Jesus Movement (with the attending rise of "Jesus Music"—the genre that eventually became known as Contemporary Christian Music, or CCM) had direct impact on many churches.

First folk music, then pop, and eventually rock 'n' roll were performed in churches. Some Christian artists began incorporating humor into their performances (most notably Daniel Amos, Ken Medema, and Steve Taylor). Still others eventually performed stand-up routines and skits of exclusively Christian-oriented material (Isaac Air Freight). Jerry Clower (1926–1998), a self-identified born-again Christian, was initially popular in the country and western market, but soon began performing in churches as well.

Outside of Taylor (who continues to write, perform, and produce superb, often funny music), the most influential of the early practitioners of the emerging Christians-who-are-funny performers was Grady Nutt (1934–1982). Nutt originally worked in Southern Baptist circles, but the ordained preacher eventually found a national audience, including regular appearances on *Hee Haw* and an eponymous network television pilot with his homespun, genuinely funny observations about what it was like to grow up Christian (or at least Southern Baptist) in the twentieth century. Like Clower, Nutt was a natural storyteller and his (now mostly out of print) LPs sold well, although nothing could match his live performances—which always ended with a readily identifiable Christian message.

Nutt's life was tragically cut short by a small plane crash at the peak of his career in 1982. His homespun stories don't translate easily to the printed page because of their length, generous use of body language, Nutt's rubbery facial expressions, and the improvisational nature of his work. Still, this excerpt on the nature of humor from his autobiography

So Good, So Far . . . captures a sliver of the genius of the man once dubbed the Prime Minister of Humor:

> Jesus was called *teacher* more often than by any other title. Humor, parable, description were the basic tools of his trade.
>
> Furthermore, humor is woven into the fabric of life just as surely as tragedy. There are tornadoes and murders and cancer. There are also surprise birthday parties, pranks, *mispronounciation*, chiggers, brushing your teeth with Brylcreem! In the midst of the awful is the absurd; in the process of frenzy there is boisterous laughter. Man causes Good Friday; then, God responds with Easter.
>
> The humorist, therefore, is *interpreter*. One who uses *this* to show *that*. One who helps you see what he or she has seen, experience what he or she has experienced, feel what he or she has felt. It is only a short step from that to *minister*. (Nutt 1979, 143)

Here Beginneth the Digression

Even the magazine sector got into the act. *The Wittenburg Door* (the misspelling of "Wittenberg" was on the magazine's original masthead and wasn't noticed by the original editors until the fourth issue . . . by which point they'd grown rather fond of it), still bills itself as "the world's pretty much only religious humor and satire magazine." Founded in 1972, by a group of youth pastors and under the guidance of Mike Yaconelli, the magazine achieved both fame and notoriety for its combination of cutting-edge interviews, single-panel cartoons and funny articles about religion. From the beginning, *The Door's* editorial mandate was to use humor and satire to hold a mirror before the church. Despite significant advances elsewhere in the arts, sciences, spirituality and microfinance, the magazine recently celebrated its thirty-fifth anniversary. (In the interests of full disclosure, I suppose it would behoove me to admit at this juncture that the author has been the Senior Editor of the magazine since 1988, a tenure that inexplicably coincides with the period of the magazine's greatest financial and spiritual decline.)

Here Endeth the Digression

M. Conrad Hyers

In recent decades, the writer who has done the most to continue the argument that genuine humor deserves a place in the pew is M. Conrad Hyers, now Professor Emeritus of Religion at Gustavus Adolphus College. Hyers' groundbreaking editing of a collection of essays on sacred humor, *Holy Laughter: Essays on Religion in the Comic Perspective* (1969), was followed by *The Comic Vision and the Christian Faith* (1981), *And God Created Laughter: The Bible as Divine Comedy* (1987), and two books on Zen Buddhism, *The Laughing Buddha: Zen and the Comic Spirit* (1989) and *Once-Born, Twice-Born Zen: The Soto and Rinzai Schools of Japanese Zen* (1989).

A well-regarded scholar—he translated Kierkegaard's difficult discourses on humor's place in the greater discussion on the intersection between the sacred and the profane (1969, 10–13)—Hyers also writes convincingly that Christians should take humor seriously in their faith lives. Hyers establishes not just the importance but the *necessity* of laughter in all facets of a Christian's life:

> Yet the ability to see the humor in things, or to create comic tales and rituals, is among the most profound and imaginative of human achievements. The comic sense is an important part of what it means to be human and humane. Without it we return to brutishness, and the Philistines are upon us. (1981, 11)

Holy Laughter is unique in other ways. Hyers carefully chose essays that cover several decades and dip into a number of philosophical, religious, and scientific traditions, and yet the book still possesses a remarkably linear flow, from Hyers' brilliantly concise introduction to an equally adroit afterword by Chad Walsh. A chapter taken from Peter L. Berger's *The Precarious Vision* seeks to reverse an erroneous presumption that has survived for a millenium and, instead, claims that—to the Christian, at least—comedy is actually more profound than tragedy:

> Tragedy can never go beyond immanence (this, incidentally, is why a Christian tragedy is a contradiction in terms). Comedy can. More than that, in a way strangely parallel to that of the Christian faith, comedy overcomes the tragic perspective. From the Christian point of view one can say that comedy, unlike tragedy, bears within it a great secret.

This secret is the promise of redemption. For redemption promises in eternity what comedy gives us in its few moments of precarious liberation—the collapse of the walls of our imprisonment. It would not be surprising if, to the blessed, redemption appears after the terrors of the world as a form of comic relief. But there can be no doubt about one thing. There will be no tragedy in heaven—by definition, as it were. But man will remain funny for ever. If nothing else there will be material for endless comedies in his relations with the angels! The tragic thus shows us man in time, but the comic may well give us an intimation of what man is and always will be, even in eternity. (Berger 1961, 214)

Hyers follows Berger's essay with a chapter from Reinhold Niebuhr's influential postwar treatise *Discerning the Signs of the Times* (1946). Niebuhr, which may surprise those who only know his monumental *The Nature and Destiny of Man* or his serious research relating Christianity to various modern realities (including politics), calls humor "a prelude to faith" and claims, "laughter is the beginning of prayer" (1946, 131). But where Berger believes that heaven rings with laughter, Niebuhr asserts that there will be no humor in the presence of the Almighty:

That is why there is laughter in the vestibule of the temple, the echo of laughter in the temple itself, but only faith and prayer, and no laughter in the holy of holies. (1946, 131)

Ultimately, Hyers charges Walsh with the unenviable task of summarizing various arguments and successfully reconciling (in my mind, at least) the apparent disconnect between Niehbur and Berger:

The comic is not a wart on the human soul but a part of the soul, and the soul is diminished if the comic is excised by any kind of spiritual X-ray. The man or woman who passes into the holy of holies and ceases to laugh is bringing into God's presence a mangled creature, one who is less than the full being that God intended him to be. The comic is an essential part of our humanity, a distinctively human trait that sets us apart from other mammals as sharply as does the cc. [cubic centimeter] content of our brains. Why should God wish comedy to go into the deep freeze just because he reveals himself? God himself is the primal humorist. The sculptor who guided evolution toward the hippopotamus has the impish playfulness of a Dada artist, and the God who chose to become man indulged in as absurd and baroque a gesture as any scientist who finds a way to turn himself into an alley cat and live among his fellow felines while still remembering the gleaming test tubes and the intellectual excitement of the laboratory.

The Christian faith is very funny. (It is also very solemn, but that is not in dispute.) It is funny because of the incongruities in it, and its total lack of monochrome dignity. (Walsh 1969, 244)

Which brings us back to the ebullient quotation from Meister Eckhart in the introduction to this volume, several dozen pages (and several hundred years) ago: "For truly, God laughs and plays."

If you've followed me through the previous 35,000 words as I've tried to build, in sometimes excruciating detail, a convincing argument as to *how* the church lost its ability to laugh and only very, very slowly regained permission to laugh, then perhaps you have a question or two yourself, such as: "Why? Why does all of this matter? And, if it *does* matter, *what*—if anything—can I do about it?"

Why and what, indeed . . .

CHAPTER 6

Carbonated Holiness

If I had to draw a picture of the person of Comedy it is so I should like to draw it: the tears of laughter running down the face, one hand still lying on the tragic page which so nearly contained the answer, the lips about to frame the great revelation, only to find it had gone as disconcertingly as a chair twitched away when we went to sit down. Comedy is an escape, not from truth but from despair: a narrow escape into faith. It believes in a universal cause for delight, even though knowledge of the cause is always twitched away from under us, which leaves us to rest on our own buoyancy. In tragedy every moment is eternity; in comedy eternity is a moment. In tragedy we suffer pain; in comedy pain is a fool, suffered gladly. —Christopher Fry (1960)

So . . .

So just what *is* this Life of Laughter we've been given permission (again) to be a part of?

It isn't silliness, although Lord knows we all could use a little more silliness in our lives. Dark and dangerous times like ours call for silliness—silliness of a positively heroic stature.

There are moments when nothing else *will* work but a great farce. The movie versions of *A Funny Thing Happened on the Way to the Forum* and *Noises Off!* are divinely silly, but should you ever get the opportunity, see them live and on stage as they were originally intended. The classic Marx Brothers films—*Duck Soup, A Night at the Opera, A Day at the Races*—are silly in the *best* sense of the word, as are the best Warner Brothers cartoons (including *What's Opera, Doc?, One Froggy Evening, Duck Dodgers in the 24 1/2th Century*, and *Duck Amuck*).

Or, if you're lucky enough, observe from a distance an exultation of young girls, generally ages 6–9, interacting in a blur of arms and legs and hair, giggly and indefatigable as young colts, shouting and dancing and preening and laughing at the sheer exhilaration of it all. This is silliness of the highest order.

But we're not talking about silliness. Silliness is hard to maintain—and rightfully so. At its best, it is spontaneous, unexpected, and refreshing like the sudden summer showers on the too-bright mornings of my Kansas childhood. Someone who is silly *all* the time, someone who never takes anything or anybody else seriously, quickly passes through the stages from Amusing to Annoying to Targeted for Slow and Painful Death . . . sometimes in a matter of minutes.

Nor are we talking about bemused cynical detachment. The great challenge of satire is to remain constantly on guard against degeneration into cynicism. Cynicism is a dead end. It is clearly marked by lazy humor with an infinite supply of easy targets. Cynicism soon evolves into self-righteous elitism. It is easy to make fun of everything. There is little wit involved. And the most easily damaged by a cynic's sneering barbs are those who can least handle it, the fragile cockeyed innocents and optimists who have become an endangered species in our postmodern world, a world that has made a god of irony.

Nope. We're not talking either extreme silliness *or* cynicism. We're stalking much more elusive big game here: *A laughing soul. A joyful spirit. A heart so full of good-natured humor that laughter just naturally spills out.*

That's not to say that everybody can do it or possess it or live it. Depression is real. In those who suffer from it, depression robs the capacity to enjoy life. It has become a modern epidemic.

That's all the more reason for Christians to work even harder to spread the joy and light and laughter of their salvation and Savior.

And yes, there are things you *can* work at . . . things you *should* work at . . . things that need to assume a bigger, more obvious part of your life. If you've come to believe that joy and light and laughter are *not* a luxury for a believer, then the next few pages may help you incorporate the core elements of a joyful, humorous outlook into your daily life.

Believe in God; Believe in Yourself

That implies, of course, that there *is* that spark of Christ-joy in you. You'll have to trust me on this—you do have one. It may be tiny, flickering, and degraded at the moment—life is hard, no question—but it ᵕ there. You were, after all, made in God's own image. If you're not sure that little spark is enough to burn into an honest-to-goodness flame, ponder the story of the feeding of the five thousand from Mark 6. Although you've probably heard this bit at least five thousand times, look at it through fresh eyes:

> Note that Jesus does not bring down manna from heaven or turn stones into food. He takes what is already there, the five loaves and two fishes, and, when it passes through Jesus' hands, there is more than enough, much more than enough, for everyone present. The point of this story is not multiplication, but distribution. The food already there is enough for all when it passes through the hands of Jesus as the incarnation of divine justice. (Borg and Crossan 2006, 115)

Marcus J. and John D. are on to something. If you're not naturally buoyant, chipper, or even happy, this insight is crucial: *God honors what you can do with what you have.* Again, I'm not downplaying the ravages of depression. I only know about it secondhand—I can't get inside someone else's skin and experience it—but I've been around enough chronically depressed people to know how debilitating it can be. For everybody else, however, the evidence of the widow and her mite alone should be enough. Jesus said what she did was enough (read Mark 12:41-44; it's in there). Meanwhile, the parable of the talents (Matt 25:14-30) does *not* apply to the distribution of humor and happiness and joyfulness.

And yet, despite all of the evidence of the Gospels to the contrary, Paul Tillich says any pastor's greatest task is to get the people of her or his church *to accept the fact that they're accepted* (1948, 162). And even more than accepted, that they're loved . . . unconditionally . . . by the flawed—but still *fabulous*—people around them and, more importantly, by the *Creator of the Whole Blamed Universe!* That knowledge may not make you want to continually laugh out loud, but you ought to at least let a little smile sneak out from time to time if you really believe it.

There's a great song, "God Believes in You," by Pierce Pettis (1998) that speaks directly to that issue:

> When your chances seem so slim, when your light burns so dim
> And you swear you don't believe in him, God believes in you.

No matter how small, useless, or overwhelmed you sometimes feel, one of the great overriding truths of the Christian faith is that God *knows* you haven't been exactly a paragon of virtue all of your life. In fact, God knows everything about you, everything you've ever thought or ever done—but *God loves you anyway*. The term we're searching for is *grace*. Or as Mike Yaconelli says:

> The grace of God is dangerous. It's lavish, excessive, outrageous, and scandalous. God's grace is ridiculously inclusive. Apparently God doesn't care who He loves. He is not very careful about the people He calls His friends or the people He calls His Church. Exactly. (Yaconelli 1998, 126)

Accept it, believe it, live it. If you do, then you'll naturally be a happier person, one who is quicker to laugh.

Friends, Community, and Church

There is just one problem with the whole "we're all in this together" church thing.

People—specifically, *other* people.

There is a legendary *Peanuts* cartoon where Linus and Lucy have been talking about professions. When Linus says he wants to become a doctor, his crabby older sister pounces:

Lucy: You a doctor! Ha! That's a big laugh. You could never be a doctor. You know why? . . . Because you don't love mankind, that's why!

Linus: I love mankind . . . it's people I can't stand!
(Schulz in Short 1965, 122)

Here's a scary thought. Did you know that *you* are on as many "can't stand" lists as there are people on *your* "can't stand" list?

In other words, you're stuck with other people. They're stuck with you. You might as well make the best of it. While the following advice from Barbara Brown Taylor was originally written for pastors, it applies to us regular people too. She says that if we're all going to get through this journey, it is really, really important for you to give a little grace to yourself *and* those around you:

Be patient with yourself, and while you are at it, be patient with the rest of us too. You cannot follow a shepherd all by yourself, after all. You are stuck with this flock, or some flock, and everyone knows that sheep are, well, sheep. They panic easily and refuse to be pushed. They make most of their decisions based on their appetites and they tend to get into head-butting contests for no reason at all. But stick with the flock. It is where the shepherd can be found, which makes it your best bet not only for survival but also for joy.

Above all, understand that you belong here, as part of the flock. (Taylor 1993, 145)

We talked about the need for community-building in the chapter on recognizing and creating humor. It is easier to surrender yourself to a joyful spirit if you are part of a community of faith. It easier to surrender to that kind of approach when you're among loving (if sometimes flawed) friends. A healthy community of faith is one that invests in the lives of the individual members. No burden is too great when it is shared by a group of loving friends. More on this later, but, as the couplet in one of my favorite hymns, "The Servant Song" by Richard Gillard (1977), goes:

I will weep when you are weeping; when you laugh, I'll laugh with you.
I will share your joy and sorrow till we've seen this journey through.

The punch line is this: Want to have a lot of laughter in your life? Find a healthy community of faith, a church, a Bible study, a Sunday school class, a group of seekers who meet regularly at the local diner for breakfast and hash out the hidden hagiographies of Habakkuk. That means, find any community that is *not* into judgment, control, condemnation, and/or fear. And once you *do* find a normal, loving, active community, get involved helping other people both inside and outside of your community.

William Sloane Coffin, as always, gives us the words that help it all fit together in this description of two well-known bodies of water in Israel, both of which are primarily filled with water from the Jordan River:

In one, fish play and roots find sustenance. In the other, there is no splash of fish, no sound of bird, no leaf around. The difference is not in the Jordan, for it empties into both, but in the Sea of Galilee: for every drop taken in one goes out. It gives and lives. The other gives nothing. And it is called the Dead Sea. (Coffin 2004, 15)

To get, you've gotta give; it's as simple as that. We're not talking about a faith justified by works theology here. This is a simple truism. You want to be happy? Help someone else because you love them, not because they deserve it. The more you're assisting someone less fortunate than yourself, the less time you spend thinking about yourself. Each time you do something like that, you're extending grace. It may be a pale, warped, weak shadow of the grace that God through Jesus Christ extends us, but it is powerful, potent grace nonetheless. William Law knew this way back in 1800:

> Our power of doing external acts of love and goodness is often very narrow and restrained. There are, it may be, but few people to whom we can contribute any worldly relief . . .
>
> You cannot heal all the sick or relieve all the poor. You cannot comfort all in distress nor be a father to all the fatherless. You cannot, it may be, deliver many from their misfortunes or teach them to find comfort in God. But if there is a love and tenderness in your heart that delights in these good works and excites you to do all that you can— if your love has no bounds but continually wishes and prays for the relief of happiness of all who are in distress—you will be received by God as a benefactor to those who have had nothing from you but your good will and tender affections. (1955, 131)

We're called to do this, in part because that Christ-love burns in ALL people, both in those who believe and in those who will someday believe. The light that emanates from that flame is valuable. All light is valuable—no, *essential*—in holding back the darkness. Former President George H. Bush Sr. got the "1,000 points of light" concept right—one candle by itself doesn't do much. But together . . .

That's why brightness on searchlights and lighthouses is measured in "candle power"—just as car engines are still compared by total horsepower. You need 'em all, one candle at a time. Light fights the darkness. Laughter fights the darkness. Laughter says, "I believe. Despite it all, I believe."

That's the Divine Comedy again.

But, as Linus has so astutely pointed out, this is all real nice in theory. You'll gain joy and happiness and laughter when you help humanity. But what about those other people who aren't just quite . . . *normal,* much less likeable? What about them?

Of course, that begs the question, "What's normal?"

Normal is *more* than "whatever gets you through the night." Normal is a bunch of otherwise disparate, unlikely, and yes—sometimes *unlikable*—people working together for both the common good and the individual good. If those criteria are met, then whatever passes for normal in *that* little community, well, *that's* normal.

Um, sounds a whole lot like church, doesn't it?

> One secret of life is that the reason life works at all is that not everyone in your tribe is nuts on the same day. Another secret is that laughter is carbonated holiness. (Lamott 2005, 65–66)

"Carbonated holiness"—what a great term! This quote comes from Anne's adventure trying to establish a Sunday School for kids at her wonderfully eclectic church in Marin County, California. Anne writes about her church a lot, about the grace that comes from the community of wildly individualistic worshipers there. People who have accepted themselves as they are, accepting other people as *they* are.

And you know what? If Anne Lamott's stories are to be believed, there is a lot of laughter in that little church! Sustaining, nurturing, silly, redemptive laughter.

For many years, the late Mike Yaconelli pastored another such church in the wilds of Yreka, California. He wrote about their joint adventures and how the battered walls often shuddered with laughter. And he wrote how, above all places he knew, save for perhaps a L'Arche community he once visited, this little church was such a place of joyful grace and redemptive, happy laughter:

> The grace of God says to you and me, "I can make last place more significant than first place. I will use prostitutes to teach others about gratitude. I will use lepers as examples of cleanliness. I will take men who persecute the church and make them its pillars. I will take the dead and give them life. I will take un-educated fishermen and make them fishers of men." God's grace does not exist to make us successful. God's grace exists to point people to a love like no other love they have ever known. (Yaconelli 1998, 130)

Grace comes from God. Grace comes from acceptance. Grace comes from community. Accepting, and then extending, grace to others is one of the ways to live a happy, laughter-filled, joyous Christian life. *Grace is doing.* If everything is firing on all cylinders, you don't just *go* to church. You *do* church.

Happiness in Heartbreak

What I'm talking about isn't some kind of hopelessly idealistic New Age concept. Nor is it another rehash of the various positive thinking credos. I'm not that smart. But I do know this: even IF you believe you are saved, even IF you believe God loves you, even IF you find a riotous, Christ-seeking bunch of goofballs who embrace you as their own; finding the humor, finding the happiness, finding the joy in life is *hard work*. It's a tough slog in a bitter, cynical, seductive world to maintain that upbeat, laughter-spiced attitude, even for a "seasoned" Christian. You've got to work at it. Daily.

But if the Easter Laugh is part of who you are, then life's worst storms will wash over you, leaving you still standing—sputtering, drenched, and shivering sometimes—but still standing.

The late E. B. White, who wrote such classics as *Stuart Little* and *Charlotte's Web*, married late in life. His wife Katherine was also a fine writer and editor, and even better known as a gardener. Their marriage was celebrated by all who knew them as one that must have been divinely inspired. And so, when it was clear that she was dying, Katherine wrote her beautiful memoir *Onward and Upward in the Garden*. Her husband wrote the introduction, including this lovely observation of her planting her beloved bulbs, even as she knew she'd never see them bloom:

> As the years went by and age overtook her, there was something comical yet touching in her bedraggled appearance on this awesome occasion—the small, hunched-over figure, her studied absorption in the implausible notion that there would be yet another spring, oblivious to the ending of her days, which she knew perfectly well was near at hand, sitting there with her detailed chart under those dark skies in dying October, calmly plotting the resurrection. (1979, xix)

There's a phrase that rolls off the tongue, "calmly plotting the resurrection." Neither Death nor Satan knew that the crucifixion wasn't the end. Katharine's October garden was deliberate in its defiance of Death. If you can laugh at Death, you can find the humor and laughter in just about anything.

Here's another example, this one from the philosopher Gillian Rose. Like Katharine, Gillian knew she was dying (of cancer) as she feverishly worked to write her autobiography, *Love's Work*, before her death in 1995. It is a glorious testament to a passionate spirit:

> [T]his sureness of self, which is ready to be unsure, makes the laughter at the mismatch between aim and achievement comic, not cynical; holy, not demonic. This is not love of suffering, but the work, the power of love, which may curse, but abides. It is power to be able *to attend*, powerful or powerless; it is love to laugh bitterly, purgatively, purgatorially, and then to be quiet. (1997, 125–26)

It is a conspiracy to cheat Death. As Rose says, "It is . . . to be able to laugh bitterly, purgatively, purgatorially, and then to be quiet." Not even Death itself will have the last laugh. We will.

If that's so, it means that laughter—purgative or just plain silly—is a powerful weapon. Norman Cousins caused a stir in medical circles with his book *Anatomy of an Illness: As Perceived by the Patient*. Cousins had been diagnosed with *ankylosing spondylitis*, among other things, and the prognosis was grim (1979, 30). But he eventually implemented an aggressive holistic self-treatment regimen that included significant time watching Marx Brothers movies and the old TV show, *Candid Camera*. The results of his "laughter therapy" were remarkable (39). Laughter as a health-promoting exercise has since been the subject of a number of studies and while the results are not always as quantifiable as its proponents would have liked, it is generally conceded to be a positive factor in both lifestyle and health, even in the most serious studies (Provine 2000, 202–203).

Laughter and a happy, positive outlook make a difference in the lives of those who laugh. Pain and heartache will come. Loss and betrayal lurk nearby. We live, after all, in a fallen world. But knowing that these things are ahead serves notice on us. Christians, armed with the knowledge that they are Supremely Loved and that their happy fate is assured, can be prepared. The joyful, confident countenance is just part of the arsenal at our disposal. Katharine White lovingly tended to her garden, Gillian Rose continued to read and write . . . and these things gave them peace and happiness. Why? Edith Wharton thinks she knows:

> In spite of illness, in spite even of the archenemy sorrow, one can remain alive long past the usual date of disintegration if one is unafraid of change, insatiable in intellectual curiosity, interested in big things, and happy in small ways. (1998, xix)

"Happy in small ways." Engaged. Empowered. Fulfilled. Again—save for those suffering from depression—happiness, joyfulness is a *choice* in a privileged society like ours. It is an action. It is not ignoring the pain or sadness around us, it is tackling them head on, boldly, *joyfully!*

Hebrews 12:1-2 says:

> Therefore, since we are surrounded by so great a cloud of witnesses, let us also lay aside every weight and the sin that clings so closely, and let us run with perseverance the race that is set before us, looking to Jesus the pioneer and perfecter of our faith, who for the sake of the joy that was set before him endured the cross, disregarding its shame, and has taken his seat at the right hand of the throne of God.

In his meditation on those verses, the late William Sloane Coffin makes a startling connection between pain and joyful laughter. We have so little joy or passion in our lives, we instinctively search for God, even if we don't know we're searching:

> It is also the joy of coming to know God, for knowledge of God is heart-felt, vital. And if God is a suffering God, if this whole universe is borne on a heart infinite in compassion, then the more we suffer in his name the closer we come to him. And the closer we come the more we are convinced that we are loved with a love far more dependable than our own, prized more highly than we could ever prize ourselves, so that like Jesus we can be full of joy, strongly invulnerable in the midst of our vulnerability. That is why to the women weeping along the way of sorrows Jesus said, "Weep for yourselves, not for me." To all appearances the incident was closed; love's boat had smashed against the daily grind. But in the eyes of faith all would be finally well. (2004, 15)

How do we know Jesus laughed? Because Jesus also suffered pain, loss, betrayal, hunger, thirst, and everything else that besets us. And because Jesus knew that "all would be finally well." It's not the laughter of the Greek and Roman gods who, from a safe distance, laughed at the travails of the poor schmucks far below Mount Olympus; it is the laughter of a fellow sufferer.

Jesus laughed because it is a good thing. Laughing—for Christian and non-Christian alike—is a catalyst, a force for good, a force for sanity.

Once again, research backs us up. In Martin Grotjahn's *Beyond Laughter*, he terms someone who strives to see the positive, humorous side of life a "humorist" and notes that the humorists are far better equipped to handle difficult situations than someone else without that approach:

> [I]n contrast to the depressive, he [the humorist] does not spend his life in grief and mourning about the milk which was spilled a long time ago; he does something about it. (1957, 55)

Grotjahn's book does not have a religious element to it (he's an M.D. from the realm of psychoanalysis), but his quote is eerily reminiscent of one of my favorite passages in the Psalms:

> You have turned my mourning into dancing;
> > you have taken off my sackcloth
> > and clothed me with joy,
> so that my soul may praise you and not be silent.
> > O LORD my God, I will give thanks to you forever. (Psalm 30:11-12)

This, by the way, leads us ever-so-nicely to the next important facet in the ongoing process to incorporate more laughter into your life and faith . . .

Play and Dancing

This is where, of course, I will probably bid adieu to my Southern Baptist readers. But play and dancing are just two more of the most visible external components of a life spent spreading joy and happiness. We've already noted Meister Eckhart's statement "God plays and laughs." And we've cited Jürgen Moltmann's *Theology of Play*. Moltmann writes in the introduction that despite the horrors in the world—from war to torture to famine—all humans *need* to play and that "it is possible that in playing we can anticipate our liberation and with laughing rid ourselves of the bonds which alienate us from real life" (1972, 3). Later, he writes that it is all part of the great design of "the Other whom we try to praise out of the depths, before whom we can rejoice and play, laugh, love, and dance, so that the chains fall away" (113).

A lot of other people think this stuff is important too. Mike Yaconelli, for instance:

> God *does* play with our souls. He hides and He seeks and His laughter heals our hearts. When God plays with us, before we know it, we are playing: playing with our neighbors, our church members, and even our families. (Yaconelli 1998, 77)

The Christian church, as you've probably noticed, has had as much difficulty with play and dance as it has had with laughter. They're all intertwined, of course. Because of our Puritan past, most of us need some kind of role model here. We've been taught for so long that "Good Christians" are somber, sober, grim, humorless, prim, and proper that we're not real good at any of these things anymore. So—who *does* dance beautifully, laugh effortlessly, and play with gleeful abandon?

Kids. Kids do it right. Always have.

Jesus loved 'em, by the way. He told us repeatedly to model ourselves after them:

> At that time the disciples came to Jesus and asked, "Who is the greatest in the kingdom of heaven?" He called a child, whom he put among

them, and said, "Truly I tell you, unless you change and become like children, you will never enter the kingdom of heaven. Whoever becomes humble like this child is the greatest in the kingdom of heaven. Whoever welcomes one such child in my name welcomes me." (Matthew 18:1-5)

Kids play, dance, and laugh, and do other such important things well because they don't take themselves too seriously. They don't become tame and muted and civilized until they've been through a few years of school and lost their wonder, excitement, and belief in Santa Claus, good witches, and talking animals. Eventually, play and dance and laughter become codified and controlled. (Dr. Seuss once wrote a book titled, *You're Only Old Once: A Book for Obsolete Children*. He could have dedicated it to any one of a number of people I know.)

Here Beginneth the Digression

Herb Gardner's brilliant *A Thousand Clowns: A Comedy in Three Acts* (1961) follows the misadventures of the gifted (though undisciplined) writer named Murray, who is again unemployed as he rebels against society's artificial norms. He has become, quite by accident, the guardian of his twelve-year-old nephew, and they are now fast friends. But Murray's bohemian lifestyle draws the attention of Child Protective Services, and a social worker comes to take the boy away. At first, Murray is worried that if they're separated, the kid will someday become a list-maker:

Murray: I didn't spend six years with him so he should turn into a list maker. He'll learn to know everything before it happens, he'll learn to plan, he'll learn how to be one of the nice dead people.

Murray is really warming up now, and Sandra, the social worker, is mesmerized:

Murray: I just want him to stay with me till I can be sure he won't turn into Norman Nothing. I want to be sure he'll know when he's chickening out on himself. I want him to get to know exactly the special thing he is or else he won't notice it when it starts to go.

By now, Murray is almost talking to himself, sadly, softly:

Murray: I will be very sorry to see him go. That kid was the best straight man I ever had. He is a laugher, and laughers are rare. I mean, you tell that kid something funny—not just any piece of corn, but something funny, and he'll give you your money's worth. It's not just funny jokes he reads, or I tell him, that he laughs at. Not just set-up funny stuff. He sees street jokes, he has the good eye, he sees subway farce and crosstown-bus humor and all the cartoons that people make by being alive. He has a good eye. And I don't want him to leave until I'm certain he'll never be ashamed of it.

Here Endeth the Digression

That said, some adult Christians might allow the idea that *play* is okay for kids and maybe . . . *just maybe* . . . certain (generally *other*) adults. Some might even agree that God has a sense of humor—how else do you explain Limburger cheese, giraffes, Paris Hilton's "fame," Donald Trump's "hair," long-eared puppies, a planet named Uranus, or the Texas legislature?

But getting adult Christians to embrace the concept of dance as an integral part of the joyous Christian life is a stretch. It's one thing for children to dance, but it's quite another for me. After all, I'm a respectable member of society. I have a reputation to uphold. I'm adult. I'm serious. Dancing? At my age? Preposterous!

And yet . . .

And yet, the Bible is chock-full of people dancing from sheer, unadulterated, unmitigated happiness. My favorite sequence is David dancing "with all his might" into Jerusalem after the return of the Ark of the Covenant, dressed only in a "linen ephod"—which was apparently the Israelite version of a Speedo bathing suit. David's wife Michal is mortified and angrily tells David so—in no uncertain terms (2 Samuel 6:1-23). This seems to be a bit snippy from someone whose husband's original bride-price to her father was a hill of Philistine foreskins—which is apparently what they did for bridal showers in those dark days before Bed, Bath & Beyond (1 Samuel 6:30).

Think, too, of Zorba's exultant dance at the end of *Zorba the Greek,* even after all of his dreams of wealth have fallen into the sea. Or the great wedding dances of dozens of nations and ethnic groups (a la *My Big Fat Greek Wedding).* And as for truly great literature, in the classic *Peanuts* episodes of decades past, Snoopy would periodically throw himself into an unrestrained dance of doggy happiness. In one well-loved cartoon strip, Snoopy exclaims, "To live is to dance." Even Lucy is swept into a couple of panels, also dancing madly. The strip ends with Snoopy still dancing and shouting, "To dance is to live!" Referring to these panels, Robert Short cites Havelock Ellis: "[Dancing] is the supreme symbol of spiritual life" because "dancing is the loftiest, the most moving, the most beautiful of the arts, because it is no mere translation or abstraction from life; it is life itself" (1965, 112).

"You turned my mourning into dancing . . . " not because we deserve it, but because God is God. It's grace.

> I know nothing, except what everyone knows—
> if there when Grace dances, I should dance.
> (Auden, 1965, 84)

What do children, Zorba the Greek, King David, and Snoopy all have in common? None of them care what other people think when they happen to laugh too loud, play too hard, or suddenly dance with unfettered abandon. They've instead abandoned themselves to the free-floating joy that pervades the universe. Most of us are too self-conscious, too self-aware to really let ourselves go. What will our neighbors think? That's why Murray's nephew in *A Thousand Clowns* is so special: "He is a laugher, and laughers are rare." My wife Mary is a laugher. She has a great, infectious, uninhibited laugh. People are instinctively drawn to her—and her laugh. (She's also a great dancer, incidentally, and no, I don't think it is a coincidence.)

So the final secret to seeing (and writing and speaking and playing and dancing) with humor is to embrace this childlike wonder of it all. Not surprisingly, Frederick Buechner gets it:

> For Christ's sake, grow up. Grow up? For old people isn't it a little too late? For young people isn't it a little too early? I do not think so. Never

too late, never too early, to grow up, to be holy. We have already tasted it after all—tasted the kindness of the Lord. (1992, 146)

And, if you're ready to make that leap, then Annie Dillard has some advice for you:

There is always an enormous temptation in all of life to diddle around making itsy-bitsy friends and meals and journeys for itsy-bitsy years on end. It is so self-conscious, so apparently moral, simply to step aside from the gaps where the creeks and winds pour down, saying, I never merited this grace, quite rightly, and then to sulk along the rest of your days on the edge of rage. I won't have it. The world is wilder than that in all directions, more dangerous and bitter, more extravagant and bright. We are making hay when we should be making whoopee; we are raising tomatoes when we should be raising Cain, or Lazarus. (Dillard 1994, 422)

Dillard's approach (and this quote is from her wonderful book *Pilgrim at Tinker Creek)* is more than just whimsy (albeit beautifully written whimsy); it is grounded in hard science. Robert R. Provine is considered one of the world's premiere experts on the psychology and biology of laughter, having written more than fifty academic articles on the topic. His scholarly (although often funny) book *Laughter: A Scientific Investigation* concludes with "Ten Tips for Increasing Laughter: Perspectives from the Mall, Workplace, and Clinic" (2000, 209–15) that echo Dillard's words. Provine provides short descriptive paragraphs after each of his Ten Tips, but the titles speak for themselves:

1. Find a friend or personable stranger.
2. The more the merrier.
3. Increase interpersonal contact.
4. Create a casual atmosphere.
5. Adopt a laugh-ready attitude.
6. Exploit the contagious laugh effect.
7. Provide humorous materials.
8. Remove social inhibitions.
9. Stage social events.
10. Tickle.

While the last entry "Tickle" probably should only be administered to someone you know really, really well, the other nine work as well in a

Christian setting as (presumably) they do in a secular one. (Special note to pastors, priests, reverends, and rabbis: Caution is strongly advised before practicing Tip #10 on your parishioners.)

While the book never mentions the church or any religious setting, I believe that Provine's research also agrees with what I have outlined in this chapter—there really are specific, concrete ways to incorporate a sense of humor into your life. His rationale is interesting:

> Ten years of prospecting taught me where to look for laughter. After the early days of trial and error, I detected underlying patterns and became more adept at predicting the social and physical settings most likely to yield laughter. Along the way, I acquired another useful insight—how to increase the laughter in our lives. Although I'm not a clinical psychologist and don't run Doctor Feelgood, Inc., it's clear that laugh enhancement is a useful enterprise. (209)

The laughter-filled life is not passive. It takes intentionality. It takes work. And the rewards are worth the effort.

> Love, like you'll never get hurt;
> You got to dance like nobody's watchin'
> (Clark and Leigh 1989, "Come From the Heart")

CHAPTER 7

It's Time for the Party to Begin

Unfortunately, this Christian Church . . . has been so largely corrupted by rank Satanism that it has become the Church where you must not laugh; and so it is giving way to that older and greater Church to which I belong: the Church where the oftener you laugh the better, because by laughter only can you destroy evil without malice, and affirm good fellowship without mawkishness. —George Bernard Shaw (1916)

In 2005, Director Niall Johnson released *Keeping Mum,* a very dark comedy starring Rowan Atkinson as the Rev. Walter Goodfellow, Kristin Scott Thomas as Gloria Goodfellow, and Maggie Smith as Grace Hawkins. As vicar of Little Wallop, Walter is excruciatingly serious and dull, Gloria is contemplating an affair, and their children are a mess. Their unhappy existence is interrupted by the arrival of Grace, their new nanny/housekeeper. Almost miraculously, their harmony (and marriage—you'll never read "The Song of Solomon" the same way again) is restored and their problems inexplicably disappear. Grace even teaches Walter to use humor in his sermons and convocation speeches, and he's successful beyond anyone's wildest dreams.

Certainly, Grace's methods aren't meant to be an object lesson in good behavior (Mary Poppins she ain't), nor is this a film for the kiddies, but the way genuine humor transforms Walter Goodfellow's formerly plodding sermons (and demeanor) rings true. He becomes a fuller, rounder, more complete human being.

Walter was a good person, just an incomplete one and therefore ineffective. Just as a single, narrow view of the Bible, while still essentially true, has become, as Walter Brueggemann says, "a truth greatly reduced":

It is a truth that has been flattened, trivialized, and rendered inane. Partly, the gospel is simply an old habit among us, neither valued nor questioned. But more than that, our technical way of thinking reduces mystery to problem, transforms assurance into certitude, revises quality into quantity, and so takes the categories of biblical faith and represents them in manageable shapes . . .

There is then no danger, no energy, no possibility, no opening for newness! . . .

That means the gospel may have been twisted, pressed, tailored, and gerrymandered until it is comfortable with technological reason that leaves us unbothered, and with ideology that leaves us with uncriticized absolutes. (1989, 1–2)

Without the freedom or ability to embrace life's lighter side in all facets of our lives, Christians have become "flattened, trivialized and rendered inane." The world already thinks we're a bunch of dour doomsayers, famous for our "thou shalt NOTS," certainly *not* for buoyant good humor and generous nature.

But if a laughing spirit really is okay, despite how the church fathers, monastics, Puritans, and others have "twisted, pressed, tailored, and gerrymandered" it to the contrary, how *do* we internalize it? Heck, how do we *externalize* it? Or even—how do we *implement* it in our lives? Besides, just because someone laughs doesn't mean they're happy. As we've seen, there are all kinds of laughter, including sardonic, proud, and cruel laughter. And happiness itself is transitory. Nobody is happy all the time. Nobody normal, that is. Life is quite content to slap us down periodically.

What we're talking about is a direct line to heaven—the Holy Spirit— that light that shines from above into our little lives and is packed with happiness, love, and laughter, like Flintstones vitamins for the soul. Someone who is filled with the Holy Spirit just laughs naturally.

You are the salt of the earth; but if salt has lost its taste, how can its saltiness be restored? It is no longer good for anything, but is thrown out and trampled underfoot. You are the light of the world. A city built on a hill cannot be hid. (Matthew 5:13-14)

(Or, as they say in the musical *Godspell* (1970), "But if that salt has lost its flavor, it ain't got much in its favor.")

Joy

That life-giving, life-affirming light, inexpressible and ineffable as it is, we've given the name . . . *joy*. C. S. Lewis intentionally titled the account of his journey from nonbeliever to believer *Surprised by Joy*. (The original title was *Surprised by a Sudden Manifestation of the Christophanic Theophany*, but a wise old editor talked him out of it.) To have regular laughter (the good kind) in your life, to have sustained happiness, you must have a joyful life.

Joy is a dicey word, though. It has been used and misused, misapplied, and misappropriated for so many unworthy causes by so many unworthy people that it has lost much of its punch. Whether from overuse or misuse, there are certain words I won't allow the students in my writing classes to use: *beautiful*, *ugly*, *great*, *tall*, *short*. *Joy* isn't one of them yet, but it is close. So it will have to do until somebody comes up with something better.

Whereas there are several different kinds of laughter, words like *rejoice* and *joy* are pretty uniform in their meaning. The trouble is, even *Webster's Ninth New Collegiate Dictionary* (I made it all the way to the final chapter before I had to consult a dictionary!) struggles to define exactly what *joy* is:

> Joy (noun): 1. a.: the emotion evoked by well-being, success, or good fortune or by the prospect of possessing what one desires: DELIGHT b.: the expression or exhibition of such emotion: GAIETY 2.: a state of happiness or felicity: BLISS 3.: a source or cause of delight. (1983, 653)

Well, *that* wasn't particularly helpful, especially in a religious context.

Rejoice is even worse. The dictionary defines it as "to give joy to" or "to feel joy or great delight" (993). Thanks a lot, Dan W.—that was *real* helpful.

So, for our purposes, *joy* will mean being so full of the peace and happiness that come from knowing the Risen Christ that it bubbles out of you. Its physical manifestations are love, laughter, and compassion, and care for those less fortunate than you. "The trading of joy comes naturally because it is of the nature of joy to proclaim and share itself. Joy cannot contain itself, as we say. It overflows" (Buechner 1992, 98).

The definition of *joy* mentioned above was cobbled together with the help of—for one last time—*The Absolute Unabashed Strongest Strong's Exhaustive Concordance of the Bible* (or, at least of the King

James Version). Earlier, we examined *mirth*, *happy*, *happiness*, *laugh*, *laughter*, *laughing*, and *laugheth* with mixed results.

But *joy* and its close cousins *joyed*, *joyful*, *joyfully*, *joyfulness*, *joying*, and *joyous* comprise nearly one full page of small, dense type (2003, 627–28).

Rejoice, *rejoiced*, *rejoiceth*, and *rejoicing* have nearly as many listings in *Strong's*—well over one hundred mentions in the Old and New Testaments (951).

I read all of the original verses to derive my opinion as to what *joy* means in a biblical context. But when I was finished, something just did not make sense to me. The Bible is, at the very least, ambivalent when it comes to *laughter* and has precious few mentions of *happiness*, and yet has hundreds of mentions of *joy* and *rejoice*. I don't get it. It would seem to me that these words would be relatively interchangeable.

Unlike the earlier chapters, there are not enough pages to parse each and every reference to either *joy* or *rejoice*, much less both of them. But there are a few verses I would like for us to consider further:

Psalm 30:5

> For his anger is but for a moment;
>   his favor for a lifetime.
> Weeping may linger for the night,
>   but **joy** comes with the morning.

Jeremiah 48:27

Permit me to interject here my favorite word in the Bible. It's found only in the King James Version (of course, the emphasis is mine).

> For was not Israel a derision unto thee? was he found among thieves?
> For since thou spakest of him, thou **skippedst** for joy.

"Skippedst"—doesn't that sound great?!

Philippians 2:1-2

> If then there is any encouragement in Christ, any consolation from love, any sharing in the Spirit, any compassion and sympathy, make my joy complete: be of the same mind, having the same love, being in full accord and of one mind.

Philippians 4:4

> Rejoice in the Lord always; again I will say, Rejoice.

1 Thessalonians 5:16

Rejoice always.

In these verses and several dozen more like them, this kind of joy endures. Rejoice *always*, the verse says. It is not a transient state, like happiness or euphoria. It permeates who you are, how you respond to people, to adversity, to life itself.

Psalm 51:12

Restore the joy of your salvation, and sustain in me a willing spirit.

There is a funny thing about the phrase "restore the joy." To restore something implies that you once had it. You had that kind of joy as a child. You *regained* it with your salvation. But in a very real sense, it has *always* been there. For whatever reasons, some perfectly legitimate, that part of your life has been repressed, beaten down, ignored, or abandoned.

Once again, I refer back to Brother Job, he of the acne, piles, boils, and pottery shards. After everything, The author of Job writes this transcendently beautiful passage about nothing less than creation itself:

> "Where were you when I laid the foundation of the earth?
>   Tell me, if you have understanding.
> Who determined its measurements—surely you know!
>   Or who stretched the line upon it?
> On what were its bases sunk,
>   or who laid its cornerstone
> when the morning stars sang together
>   and all the heavenly beings shouted for joy?" (Job 38:4-7)

Please know that when you received Jesus Christ into your life, not only did the cherubim and seraphim sing, but the prophets were giddy with delight, the saints (led by St. Vitus) danced, and the Archangel Michael laughed at Lucifer—to his face. This joyous cacophony is repeated every time *any* sinner repents or any child professes Christ. Heaven's a fun place. Lots of laughs. Nary a harp in sight. (Lots of accordions, though. It is my considered opinion that you just naturally find accordions and happy people together.) "Cosmos has been victorious over chaos, faith over doubt, trust over anxiety; and man is now truly free to laugh with the laughter of higher innocence. Humor becomes the play of joy" (Hyers 1969, 239).

This is what we were missing long before we knew we were searching for it. Some people have called it the "God-shaped vacuum" in our lives—to have (or regain) the joy of our salvation. Alas, most of us set miserably meager goals for ourselves. "I just want to be happy," you might say. Or, "I just want to be appreciated for who I am." But Jesus Christ wants so much more for us.

Frederick Buechner says we should constantly remind ourselves of the source of *all* good things; that "joy is not the same as happiness" (1969, 101). After all, you can do things that will make you temporarily happy. You can—quite undeservedly, in my case—find yourself in a great, nurturing relationship, living in a waterproof house with Bose speakers in every room. (Well, actually, I'm still waiting on the speakers.) You can even fall into a fulfilling, reasonably well-paying job. Hey, it could happen . . .

But those indefinable moments of joy when the veil between heaven and earth is temporarily pierced—those we shouldn't take credit for. Any reasonable person knows that those moments are of heavenly origin. They are so achingly beautiful that you wish you could capture them in a bottle, like a summer firefly, and keep them forever. Those moments come from, as Buechner says, ". . . the unspeakable joy . . . of just being alive" (102).

This "unspeakable joy," which can inhabit both the body and the flesh, is not some kind of mystical, impossible goal. It is available to us *now*:

> [J]oy is always all-encompassing; there is nothing of us left over to
> hate with or to be afraid with, to feel guilty with or to be selfish about.

Joy is where the whole being is pointed in one direction, and it is something that by its nature a man never hoards but always wants to share . . . Joy is a mystery because it can happen anywhere, anytime, even under the most unpromising circumstances, even in the midst of suffering, with tears in its eyes. Even nailed to a tree. (102)

Here's a bonus. If you're a believer and believe you're called to spread the message, what's the best form of evangelism? Is it massive, faceless rallies where people are whipped to frenzy by an evangelist who then flies out of town on Friday? Or is it *to possess this inexplicable* joy *and have it permeate who you are in your dealings with all other people?* If it shines through you, then other people will instinctively want what you have. They'll be drawn to you. Studies have repeatedly shown that *that's* the most effective kind of evangelism.

I'll bet you already know somebody like that. They're laughers. They're givers. They're lovers.

I'm not really qualified to write much about the *giving* and *loving* part of that equation (besides, the book is titled *Jesus Laughed: The Redemptive Power of Humor*), but I believe I *can* help with the *laughing* stuff.

Chapter 1 was a shortened version of the class (and occasionally longer seminar) I teach on recognizing and writing with humor. Knowing those precepts—Surprise, Commonality and Community, Always Aim Up, and Artful Elaboration—will help you *live* with humor as well.

But first, and you'll have to trust me on this, if you want the Gift of Laughter, then you must make it a *habit*. Any habit—from jogging to smoking—takes repetition to integrate it into your lifestyle. A couple dozen repetitions, at least right at first. This is serious stuff. You've got to work at it, cultivate it, pray for it, practice it. Not in the manner of a bad comedian practicing jokes from the Internet on a sparsely attended open mic night at the local Kristian Komedy Klub, but employing ALL of the elements and intentionality of humor and joy we've discussed throughout the book.

Surprise

To live with surprise, you must be open to surprise. You must put yourself in a position to be surprised. A mind-numbing routine at work or school or even play will kill it. *Bird by Bird* is Anne Lamott's very funny book on writing. And—surprise—the process of becoming a creative writer is very similar to the process of becoming a fully rounded, loving, laughing human being:

> There is ecstasy in paying attention. You can get into a kind of Wordsworthian openness to the world, where you see in everything the essence of holiness, a sign that God is implicit in all of creation. Or maybe you are not predisposed to see the world sacramentally, to see everything as an outward and visible sign of inward, invisible grace. This does not mean that you are worthless Philistine scum. Anyone who wants to can be surprised by the beauty or pain of the natural world, of the human mind and heart, and can try to capture just that—the details, the nuance, what is. (1995, 100–101)

Everything is inherently funny when you think about it, just as everything is sacred, including Philistine scum. Be aware of all of God's creation—both the beauty of it and (sometimes) the humor of it. Think back again to Murray's amazing nephew in *A Thousand Clowns:* "He sees street jokes, he has a good eye, he sees subway farce and crosstown-bus humor and all the cartoons people make by being alive."

Sure, that kid might have been born with the gift, but Murray nurtured it. Nurture both in yourself and in others what Mike Yaconelli calls the "dangerous wonder" of life (1998). "As that which is grounded in the sacred, humor is also the laughter within the joy of faith" (Hyers, 1969, 238–39).

Community and Commonality

Even if this doesn't come naturally to you, if you work really hard, you'll find what is sacred *and* funny in God's creation. Once that becomes second nature, work just as hard to find a like-minded community to share your search (if you're not already in one). I don't know what will work for you. For me, it has always been church. If you're a Christian and you're not in a fellowship with other believers, then you should probably be looking for such a group . . . no matter how many times you've been burned by failed and toxic churches and preachers in the past. I hate to belabor something you probably already know, but Jesus was *real* big on this whole community thing, loving your neighbor, and helping each other. Funny, life-affirming people like that are always good friends too. They invest in each other. Once again, William Sloane Coffin says it well:

For joy is to escape from the prison of selfhood and to enter by love into union with the life that dwells and sings within the essence of every other thing and in the core of our own souls. Joy is to feel the doors of the self fly open into a wealth that is endless because none of it is ours and yet it all belongs to us. (2004, 122–23)

You want to escape from the "prison of self-hood?" Do something nice for someone else. You want friends? Be a friend. You want to be included in the life of a good, happy church? Get involved in the life of that church. There's always something that needs doing in churches. Do that, and the friends will come (in normal churches, anyway). You make *real* friends a lot easier by working with people than by partying with them.

And those kinds of friends make great listeners. They're invested in your life. If you're a budding funny guy or gal, they'll be a great audience—laughing at all of the right places. And if you're struggling through a rough patch in your life, they'll be there to help you along the way.

Here Beginneth the Final Digression

It must be hard to be a pastor. Most pastors—for many reasons, some of them very good—feel they can't really be a part of their congregations. You make a few close friends and other people start sulking because you're playing "favorites." You try to treat everyone equally, being warm and friendly but with a certain reserve and certain boundaries—then people start saying you're aloof and standoffish. It's a delicate—probably dang near impossible—balance. Check out the comment of Jesus in Matthew:

> For John came neither eating nor drinking, and they say, "He has a demon"; the Son of Man came eating and drinking, and they say, "Look, a glutton and a drunkard, a friend of tax collectors and sinners!" Yet wisdom is vindicated by her deeds. (Matthew 11:18-19)

Man, it'd probably have been easier if a pastor had gone into brain surgery instead of preaching, like mom had wanted.

Here Endeth the Final Digression

And it is no secret that people naturally gravitate to individuals who are fun to be around. If you're genuinely funny and loving and honest, people will find you. The good churches are filled with people like this, because they're all (more or less) on the same page, working toward the same end, involved (in a good way) in each other's lives, helping each other, providing a safe place to rest and cry and laugh.

If the group you're in, whether it is a church or some other informal assemblage of people, is NOT like that, *then leave it.* Yesterday. And find one that is, and get involved there. You'll never find happiness and genuine laughter where you are.

Besides, on a pragmatic note, churches are just great places to find funny stuff. Mission trips, Sunday school, vacation Bible school, choir, potluck suppers, Meals on Wheels, youth camp, and Wednesday night fellowship all provide fodder for a thousand stories, stories you won't find by staying home night after night watching *Saved by the Bell* or *American Idol* reruns.

Artful Elaboration (or, if you must, Exaggeration)

Okay, this one gets tricky. For storytelling, it is essential. But in life, I'm using my editorial discretion to look at this concept from another point of view entirely. Truth is truth, right? But to convey truth, sometimes you need to bring it into sharper focus.

A good story isn't *everything* that happened. A good story is everything *interesting* that happened, as well as everything that the storyteller consciously *chose* to include to make a certain point. Give two authors or two screenwriters the exact same original material and you'll get radically different results. (I talk about this at length in *Reluctant Prophets and Clueless Disciples: Introducing the Bible by Telling Its Stories.*)

But truth is finite. Unchanging. Absolute. Or is it? My first day of class at Baylor University in 1972, I was fortunate to have the legendary David McHam teaching my introductory journalism class. He was lecturing normally when, suddenly, two boys who had been whispering loudly in the back of the class started pushing each other. Their whispers turned to shouts. At last, one of the boys took a swing at the other, and a full-fledged fight ensued. The larger boy grappled the first boy to the ground and—before any of us could respond—they rolled out into the hall, still wrestling angrily. We were shocked, frozen in place.

126

A heartbeat later, the two walked back in, laughing. McHam applauded and said to the class, "Okay, write up what just happened. You have thirty minutes."

Thirty minutes later, he read our accounts. *All twenty of our versions of what happened right before our eyes differed, sometimes significantly.* That's what the police face every day. There is an accident or a robbery and none of the eyewitnesses can agree on what happened, when it happened, why it happened, how it happened, or even who it happened to.

I know *I* told the truth that day in McHam's class . . . at least, I told the truth as I saw and heard it.

Storytelling of all kinds—particularly if it involves humor—requires the storyteller to assemble a narrative from thousands of possible facts and opinions, organize them, eliminate most of them, and present the finished tale to the listener. Is this somehow less true than if the story-teller had just recounted an event or conversation verbatim, employing hour upon hour of minute detail? We all know someone whose stories drag on forever. How much do you actually retain from those frightfully exact stories (other than the feeling that your life is slipping away from you and this is an hour you'll never, *ever* get back)?

In this context, Artful Elaboration means highlighting, spotlighting, colorizing the essentials.

Jesus told parables, little stories with a point. Sometimes they were about pedestrian things—farming, sheep herding, a lost brother, a lost coin, a mustard seed. But sometimes he talked about camels squeezing through the eye of a needle or Lincoln logs in the eye of the beholder.

Jesus always told the truth. He just told it in different ways.

Truth-telling is a dangerous business. For centuries, fools and jesters used humor and satire to tell the king unpleasant truths. In England until the mid-nineteenth century, it was difficult to conduct any investigative reporting because the law said "the greater the truth the greater the libel" (Columbia 2001–2005). It was because of that legal precedent—and the fear of jail—that many of England's greatest writers turned to humor and satire to make their points. One famous quote is apocryphally credited to Oscar Wilde, who faced the wrath of the English judicial system and only barely survived his stay in Reading jail:

> If you want to tell people the truth, make them laugh,
> otherwise they'll kill you. (Wilde, n/d)

And the little boy who shouted that the emperor has no clothes? I suspect the suppressed versions of the story have him being whisked away by the emperor's palace guard, drawn and *sixteenthed* (which hurts four times as much as being drawn and quartered).

My punch line is this—you want to change things? Using humor to tell the truth is one effective way to do it. You can (generally) get away with a lot more.

Larger than Life Is Funny

A second point. If you want people to *remember* a truth, be honest—but tell that truth larger than life-size. In fact, the more honest you are, the bigger you need to tell it.

The past master of this is Anne Lamott. As a writer, I find myself turning repeatedly to her book on the writing process, *Bird by Bird*, both because of its brutal honesty and because of her knack for Artful Elaboration. In this scene, Anne has sent her latest novel to her agent with her usual trembling trepidation and has heard nothing for a week:

> And then you see in a flash of blinding insight that your agent and editor are in cahoots, and what you heard as irritation was really just the strain of withholding hysterics. After being on the phone all morning reading each other passages from your book, they agree that it is the most embarrassingly bad book ever written, and they are honking and screaming with laughter. At one point your editor is laughing so hard that she has to take some digitalis, and your agent ruptures a blood vessel in his throat. They are reading the scene to each other where your hero's father dies. (1995, 210)

The emotions Anne conveys during these trying times are absolutely, drop-dead, on-target true. That's how this writing biz *really* is. Believe me, those descriptions are much more true than if she'd written, "The time between mailing the manuscript and its acceptance by a publisher is a challenging one for most writers."

It's very, very funny because it *is* true, even if the agent really hasn't ruptured a blood vessel or she really doesn't look like Orson Welles. Artful Elaboration.

How this plays out in your daily life is this: Live Large. Few people want to hear the umpteenth retelling of your problems with your pointy-haired boss, or your various physical ailments, or the absolute latest most darling thing your kitty-witty did last night on the heirloom quilt. Instead, be interesting and be interested in other people. Do interesting things. Talk about these things. Listen with genuine attention to others talk about *their* lives. Laugh at the right places. Applaud, if necessary. Be engaged. Be funny. Tell stories. Use Artful Elaboration (and remember to Always Aim Up or make yourself the brunt of your stories). Stay upbeat, even when you don't feel like it. Elmo and Big Bird have more friends than Oscar the Grouch.

This *doesn't* mean be the "life of the party," the guy who runs around with a lampshade on his head and drinks too much and laughs uproariously at his own rambling stories. Don't be that guy (or gal).

And this isn't the same as being the class clown or your fellow employee who doesn't take his job (or anything) seriously as he stands around the water cooler telling jokes, forcing you (and everybody else) to work harder because he's slacking off. Don't be that guy (or gal), either.

Instead, be alive. And one of the great things about being truly alive is that God has given us a pretty wonderful—and pretty funny—place to call our own for a while. For Christians, *all* of life is a party:

> The more pagan a society becomes, the more boring its people become. The sign that Jesus is in our hearts, the evidence of the truth of the Gospel is . . . *we still have a light on in our souls*. We still have a gleam in our eye. We are alive, never boring, always playful, exhibiting in our everydayness the "spunk" of the Spirit. The light in our souls is not some pietistic somberness, it is the spontaneous, unpredictable love of life. Christians are not just people who live godly lives, we are people who know how to *live* period. Christians are not just examples of moral purity, we are also people filled with a bold mischievousness. Christians not only know how to practice piety, we also know how to party. I believe it's time for the party to begin. (Yaconelli 1989, 40)

Remember the arresting parable—the one that involves a rich man who throws an elaborate feast for all of the town's Big Shots (Luke 14:15-24, see chapter 3)? When none of them show up, he tells his servants to compel people from prisons, hospitals, and substance abuse rehab centers, along with the poor, the crippled, and the blind—in short, everybody else—to come to the banquet table. Imagine the surprise of all of these poor, hungry souls as they tentatively wander in and see the massive tables groaning with the tastiest food imaginable. Imagine the wild party that must have followed!

We are the poor souls. The world, the life that Christ has given us, is the banquet. Why aren't we laughing and having a jolly good time? Is it because we think we don't deserve the feast? Forget what the Puritans say; we're children of the King!

If you still don't believe this, think for a moment about Jacob. This guy lied, stole, and cheated—friends, foe, and family alike—and yet God still made this con-man father of the Twelve Tribes of Israel. There's a lesson there:

> [L]uckily for Jacob, God doesn't love people because of who they are but because who he is. *It's on the house* is one way of saying it and *it's by grace* is another . . . (Buechner 1979, 58)

You can't possibly live out all of the Ten Commandments (besides the fact that there are actually several dozen of them, not just ten). Nobody's perfect. That's okay; God took that little fact into account a long time ago: "Most people believe that following Jesus is all about living *right. Not true.* Following Jesus is all about living *fully*" (Yaconelli, 1998, 94).

What a Ride!

Finally, what if this is all wrong? What if people like Mike Yaconelli, Anne Lamott, Frederick Buechner, Conrad Hyers, William Sloane Coffin, and the others have it backward? What if this business about striving earnestly for a life full of joy and happiness is nothing more than gallows humor—and St. Augustine, Tertullian, Increase Mather, and the rest of the Religious Gloom Squad are right? What if our God *is* an angry and vengeful God, waiting, watching to doom us for all eternity for the slightest misstep, including laughter—*especially* laughter.

Or, nearly as bad, what if there is no God, as the new atheists say. What if they're right?

In response, permit me to first cite short passages from two books, one scientific and one academic. I have no idea if Martin Grotjahn (*Beyond Laughter*) or Erich Segal (*The End of Comedy*) are believers. I hope they are, but there is nothing in either book that would lead me to that conclusion.

> Everything done with laughter helps us to be human. Laughter is a way of human communication which is essentially and exclusively human. It can be used to express an unending variety of emotions. It is based on guilt-free release of aggression, and any release makes us perhaps a little better and more capable of understanding one another, ourselves, and life. What is learned with laughter is learned

well. Laughter gives freedom, and freedom gives laughter. He who understands the comic begins to understand humanity and the struggle for freedom and happiness. (Grotjahn 1957, viii–ix)

—∿—

The essential human comedy is an odyssey from estrangement abroad to reunion at home. And the happiest of Happy Endings is… laughter in the house. (Segal 2001, 26)

Mike Yaconelli used a roller coaster model of Christianity for many years in his books and during his extraordinarily funny/real talks to youth pastors and youth workers. The Christian life, he said, was like a roller coaster, jostling around from side to side, upside-down, picking up speed, then hurtling into another loop. He made it sound like a *good* thing. It's called *passion*. It's called being fully alive. Mike laughed more than anybody I know, save for my wife Mary, who (as I said earlier) is one of the world's great, gracious laughers. As for Mike, whose life was taken from us far too soon a few years ago, I honestly believe that this excerpt is actually what happened in those final seconds before he met the Savior he'd followed for so many years:

> I often say to people, "If I were to have a heart attack right at this moment, I hope I would have just enough air in my lungs and just enough strength in me to utter one last sentence as I fell to the floor: 'What a ride!' My life has been up and down, careening left then right, full of mistakes and bad decisions, and if I died right now, even though I would love to live longer, I could say from the depths of my soul, 'What a ride!'" (1998, 93–94)

What has your life been like? A roller coaster? Have you gripped the rollbar with clenched knuckles, slammed your eyes shut, and disembarked trembling with fear? Or have you howled and hollered with every hairpin turn, laughing as the ride made that last, long, (probably) suicidal descent before leveling out? Have you embraced the passion or fought it?

Becoming a *laugher*—becoming someone who embodies the joyful freedom that our salvation gives us to such a degree that we spontaneously break out in gales of laughter (or at least little drizzles of giggles) from time to time—may not be the end-all and be-all of life.

But it ain't a bad start, either . . .

"Restore the joy of your salvation . . ." Come like a little child again, trusting, honest, and open to the One who continually greets you with open arms: "I have said these things to you so that *my joy* may be in you, and that *your joy* may be complete" (John 15:11). *That's* what Jesus wants for our lives. And that's what we need to be sharing, spreading, like light in the darkness, in our churches, in our lives.

Oh, and one other thing . . . MAKE 'EM LAUGH!

Resource List

Adkin, Neil. 1985. The Fathers on Laughter, *Orpheus* 6:149–50.

Alighieri, Dante. 1893. *The Divine Comedy of Dante Alighieri*. Translated by Henry Wadsworth Longfellow. London: George Routledge and Sons.

Allen, Woody. 1971. *Getting Even*. New York: Random House.

Allen, Woody, and Marshall Brickman. 1977. *Annie Hall*. Film. Transcribed by the author.

Armstrong, Regis J., J. A. Wayne Hellmann, and William J. Short. 1999–2002. *Francis of Assisi: Early Documents*, 3 vols. and index. New York: New City Press.

Aschkenasy, Nehama. 2006. The Book of Ruth as Comedy: Classical and Modern Perspectives, *Scrolls of Love: Ruth and the Song of Songs*. Edited by Peter S. Hawkins and Lesleigh Cushing Stahlberg. New York: Fordham University Press.

Asher, Ralph. 2005. Who's Afraid of Martin? (Interview with Martin Marty), *The Wittenburg Door* 197 (January–February): 19.

Auden, W. H. 1965. Whitsunday in Kirchstetten, *About the House*. New York: Random House.

Barclay, Robert. 1678 (1st English edition). *An Apology for True Christian Divinity as the Same is Held Forth and Preached by the People, in Scorn, Called Quakers. Being a Full Explanation and Vindication of Their Principles and Doctrines, by Many Arguments Deduced from Scripture and Right Reason, and the Testimonies of Famous Authors, Both Ancient and Modern, with a Full Answer to the Strongest Objections Usually Made Against Them*. (1886. 14th edition published in London: R. Barclay Murdoch).

Barth, Karl, and Geoffrey William Bromiley. 1975. *The Doctrine of the Word of God: Prolegomena to Church Dogmatics, vol. 2, part 1*. Edinburgh: T. & T. Clark.

Baudelaire, Charles. 1965. On the Essence of Laughter, *Comedy: Meaning and Form*. Edited by Robert W. Corrigan. San Francisco: Chandler Publishing Company.

Berger, Peter L. 1961. *The Precarious Vision*. Garden City, N.Y.: Doubleday.

Blakney, Raymond Bernard. 1941. *Meister Eckhart: A Modern Translation*. New York: Harper & Brothers.

Borg, Marcus J., and John Dominic Crossan. 2006. *The Last Week: The Day-by-Day Account of Jesus's Final Week in Jerusalem*. San Francisco: HarperSanFrancisco.

Brown, Robert McAffee. 1963. *Portrait of Karl Barth*. From the introduction by Georges Casalis. Garden City, N.Y.: Doubleday.

Brueggemann, Walter. 1989. *Finally Comes the Poet: Daring Speech for Proclamation*, Minneapolis: Fortress Press.

Buechner, Frederick. 1969. *The Hungering Dark*. New York: The Seabury Press.

———. 1979. *Peculiar Treasures: A Biblical Who's Who*. San Francisco: Harper & Row.

———. 1992. *The Clown in the Belfry*. San Francisco: HarperSanFrancisco.

Callimachus. n/d. From address by Desmond Egan, Poet and Artistic Director of the Gerard Manley Hopkins Society in Kilbelin Cemetary (Kildare) at the funeral of Irish Sculptor, James McKenna on October 13, 2000 (http://www.gerardmanleyhopkins.org/sculptor/address.html).

Chesterton, Gilbert K. 1909. *Orthodoxy*. London: John Lane Company.

———. 2001. *St. Francis of Assisi*. London: Continuum International Publishing. (Orig. pub. 1924, London: Hodder and Stoughton Ltd.)

Chrysostom, John. 1843. *The homilies of S. John Chrysostom, archbishop of Constantinople, on the first epistle of St. Paul the apostle to the Corinthians*. Oxford: John Henry Parker.

Clark, Susanna, and Richard Leigh. 1989. "Come from the Heart" on Kathy Mattea, *Willow in the Wind*. Polygram Records. Song.

Coffin, William Sloane. 2004. *Credo*. Louisville: Westminster John Knox Press.

Columbia Encyclopedia, The. 2001–05. 6th Edition. Columbia University Press. http://www.Bartleby.com/65/pr/press-fr.html (accessed online 2007).

Cousins, Norman. 1979. *Anatomy of an Illness as Perceived by the Patient: Reflections on Healing and Regeneration*. New York: W. W. Norton & Company.

Covici, Pascal, Jr. 1997. *Humor and Revelation in American Literature: The Puritan Connection*. Columbia: University of Missouri Press.

Cox, Harvey. 1969. *The Feast of Fools: A Theological Essay on Festivity and Fantasy*. Cambridge: Harvard University Press.

DeVille, Adam A. J. 2004. In Defense of Christian Snobbery: The Case of Evelyn Waugh Reconsidered, *Latin Mass: A Journal of Catholic Culture* (Spring): 73–74.

Dillard, Annie. 1994. *The Annie Dillard Reader*. New York: HarperCollins.

Dostoevsky, Fyodor. 1949. *The Brothers Karamazov*. New York: The Heritage Press.

Eco, Umberto. 1983. *The Name of the Rose*. San Diego: Harcourt Brace Jovanovich. Screenplay adaptation by Andrew Birkin, Gerard Brach, Howard Franklin, and Alain Godard (1986). Dialogue transcribed by author.

Edwards, Jonathan. 2005. *Sermons of Jonathan Edwards*. Peabody, Mass: Hendrickson.

Elliott, R.C. 1965. The Satirist and Society, *Comedy: Meaning and Form*. Edited by Robert W. Corrigan. San Francisco: Chandler Publishing Company.

Ferry, David, translator. 2001. *The Epistles of Horace*. New York: Farrar, Strauss and Giroux.

Fosdick, Harry Emerson. 1915. *The Manhood of the Master*. New York: Association Press.

Foster, Benjamin A. 1992. Mesopotamia, *Anchor Bible Dictionary*. Edited by David Noel Freedman. New York: Doubleday.

Frank, Anne. 1959. *The Works of Anne Frank*. Introduction by Ann Birstein and Alfred Kazin. Westport, Conn.: Greenwood Press.

Frank, P. S. 1964. *Angelikus Bios*. Munster, Westfalen: Aschendorffsche, Verlagsbuchhandlung.

Fry, Christopher. 1960. Comedy, *The Tulane Drama Review* 4 (March) 3:77.

Gardner, Herb. 1961. *A Thousand Clowns: A Comedy in Three Acts*. New York: Samuel French.

Gilhus, Ingvild Saelid. 1997. *Laughing Gods, Weeping Virgins*. London: Routledge.

Gillard, Richard. 1977. "The Servant Song." San Clemente, Calif.: Maranatha Music. As performed by Bukas Palad on *God of Silence*. Quezon City, Philippines: Jesuit Communications Foundation. Song Lyrics.

Grotjahn, Martin. 1957. *Beyond Laughter*. New York: McGraw-Hill.

Hall, Michael G. 1988. *The Last American Puritan: The Life of Increase Mather 1639–1723*. Middletown, Conn: Wesleyan University Press.

Hamilton, William. 1959. Humor: Plausible and Demonic, *The Christian Century* (July): 807.

Hastings, Max, editor. 1985. *The Oxford Book of Military Anecdotes*, Oxford, England: The Oxford University Press.

Hazlitt, William. 1901. On Wit and Humor, *Lectures on the English Poets and the English Comic Writers*. London: George Bell and Sons.

Hobbes, Thomas. 1931. *Leviathan*. Everyman's Library Edition. Translated by A. D. Lindsay. London: J. M. Dent & Sons (originally published in 1651).

Hyers, Conrad M. 1969. *Holy Laughter: Essays on Religion in the Comic Perspective,* New York: The Seabury Press.

———. 1981. *The Comic Vision and the Christian Faith*. New York: The Pilgrim Press.

James, John Angell. 1847. *An Earnest Ministry: The Want of the Times*. Edinburgh, Scotland: Banner of Truth Trust (reprinted 1993).

Kammen, Michael. 1993. *Mystic Chords of Memory: The Transformation of Tradition in American Culture*. New York: Vintage Books. (See especially chapters 7 and 12.)

Lambert, W. 1960. *Babylonian Wisdom Literature*. London: Oxford University Press.

Lamott, Anne. 1995. *Bird by Bird: Some Instructions on Writing and Life*. New York: Anchor Books.

————. 2005. Holy of Holies 101, *Plan B: Further Thoughts on Faith*. New York: Riverhead Books.

Langer, Susanne K. 1953. *Feeling and Form: A Theory of Art*. New York: Charles Scribner's Sons.

Lattey, C., editor. 1928. *The Spiritual Exercises of St. Ignatius*. St. Louis, Mo.: B. Herder Book Co.

Laude, Patrick. 2005. *Divine Play, Sacred Laughter, and Spiritual Understanding*. New York: Palgrave MacMillan.

Law, William. 1955. *A Serious Call to a Devout and Holy Life*. Philadelphia: The Westminster Press.

Lewis, C. S. 1955. *The Magician's Nephew*. New York: Macmillan.

————. 1978. *The Lion, the Witch and the Wardrobe*. New York: Collier Books.

————. 2001. *The Screwtape Letters with Screwtape Proposes a Toast*. San Francisco: HarperSanFrancisco.

Macdonald, George. 1871. *The Miracles of Our Lord*. Edited by Rolland Hein. Wheaton, Ill: Harold Shaw Publishers. Reprinted 1980.

Meltzer, Edmund S. 1992. Ancient Egypt, *Anchor Bible Dictionary,* vol. 3. Edited by David Noel Freeman. New York: Doubleday.

Mencken, H. L. 1927. *A Book of Prefaces*. Garden City, N.Y.: Garden City Publishing.

————. 1949. *A Mencken Chrestomathy*. New York: Alfred A. Knopf.

Merriam-Webster. 1983. *Webster's Ninth New Collegiate Dictionary*. Springfield, Mass.: Merriam-Webster.

Migliore, Daniel L. 1986. Reappraising Barth's Theology, *Theology Today* 43, no. 3 (October).

Moltmann, Jürgen. 1972. *Theology of Play*. Translated by Reinhard Ulrich. New York: Harper & Row.

Moltmann, Jürgen, and Elisabeth Moltmann-Wende. 2003. *Passion for God: Theology in Two Voices*. Louisville, Ky.: Westminster John Knox Press.

Morreall, John. 1999. *Comedy, Tragedy, and Religion*. Albany: State University of New York Press.

Musa, Mark. 2003. *The Portable Dante*. Translated, edited, and with an Introduction and Notes by Mark Musa. New York: Penguin Books.

Niebuhr, Reinhold. 1946. *Discerning the Signs of the Times: Sermons for Today and Tomorrow*. New York: Charles Scribner's Sons.

Nietzsche, Friedrich. 1956. In *Existentialism from Dostoevsky to Sartre*. Edited and translated by Walter Kaufman. New York: Meridian Books.

————. 2004. Quoted in *New Blackfriars* vol. 85, no. 996 (March): 259.

Nutt, Grady. 1979. *So Good, So Far. . . .* Nashville: Impact Books.

O'Connor, Flannery. 1964. The Violent Bear It Away, *Three*. New York: The New American Library.

Pettis, Pierce. 1998. "God Believes in You," *Everything Matters*. Compass Records. http://s98119973.onlinehome.us/ppdiscog/discog/trackdetails/track4228_lyrics.html (Accessed 2007). Song lyrics.

Pope, Alexander, translator. 1899. *The Iliad of Homer*. New York, Macmillan & Company.

Provine, Robert R. 2000. *Laughter: A Scientific Investigation*. New York: Penguin Books.

Pusey, Edward B., translator. 1909. *Confessions of St. Augustine, Second Book*. New York: P. F. Collier & Son.

Reid, Barbara E. 2003. The Acts of the Apostles, *The New Interpreter's Study Bible*. Edited by Leander E. Keck. Nashville: Abingdon Press.

Resnick, I. M. 1987. *Risus Monasticus*: Laughter and Medieval Monastic Culture, *Revue Benedictine* vol. 97, no. 97:90–100.

Rose, Gillian. 1997. *Love's Work*. London: Vintage.

Russo, Richard, and Niall Johnson, screenwriters. 2005. *Keeping Mum*. A Tusk Production.

Schaff, Philip, editor. 1956. Saint Chrysostom: Homilies on the Gospel of St. John and the Epistles to the Hebrews vol. 14, *A Select Library of the Nicene and Post-Nicene Fathers of the Christian Church*. Grand Rapids, Mich.: Wm. B. Eerdmans Publishing.

———. 1956. Saint Chrysostom: on the priesthood; ascetic treatises; selected homilies and letters; homilies on the statutes vol. 9, *A Select Library of the Nicene and Post-Nicene Fathers of the Christian Church*. Grand Rapids, Mich.: Wm. B. Eerdmans Publishing.

Scullard, H. H. 1981. *Festivals and Ceremonies of the Roman Republic*. Ithaca, N.Y.: Cornell University Press.

Segal, Eric. 2001. *The Death of Comedy*. Cambridge, Mass.: Harvard University Press.

Shaw, George Bernard. 1916. *Dramatic Opinions and Essays with an Apology by Bernard Shaw* vol. 1, New York: Brentano's.

Short, Robert L. 1965. *The Gospel According to Peanuts*. Richmond, Va.: John Knox Press.

Stanhope, Philip Dormer. 1847. *The Letters of Philip Dormer Stanhope, Earl of Chesterfield; including numerous letters now first published from the original manuscripts, edited, with notes, by Lord Mahon* vol. 1. London: Richard Bentley.

Strong, James, John R. Kohlenberger III, and James A. Swanson, editors. 2001. *The Strongest Strong's Exhaustive Concordance of the Bible*. Grand Rapids, Mich.: Zondervan.

Taylor, Barbara Brown. 1993. *The Preaching Life*. Cambridge, Mass.: Cowley Publications.

Tertullian. 1941. Quoted by Blaise Pascall in *Pensées: The Provincial Letters*. Translated by Thomas M'Crie. New York: The Modern Library.

———. 1959. *Disciplinary, Moral and Ascetical Works*. Translated by Rudolph Arbesmann, Sister Emily Joseph Daley, and Edwin A. Quain. New York: Fathers of the Church, Inc.

Tillich, Paul. 1948. *The Shaking of the Foundations*. New York: Charles Scribner's Sons.

———. 1951. *Systematic Theology* vol. 1. Chicago: University of Chicago Press.

———. 1955. *The New Being*. New York, Charles Scribner's Sons.

Todd, John M. 1982. *Luther: A Life*. New York: The Crossroad Publishing Company.

Trueblood, Elton. 1964. *The Humor of Christ*. New York: Harper & Row.

Walsh, Chad. 1969. On Being with It: An Afterword, *Holy Laughter: Essays on Religion in the Comic Perspective*. Edited by Conrad M. Hyers. New York: The Seabury Press.

Warner, Marina. 1976. *Alone of All Her Sex: The Myth and the Cult of the Virgin Mary*. New York: Alfred E. Knopf.

Wharton, Edith. 1998. *A Backward Glance*. New York: Simon & Schuster.

Whedbee, J. William. 1977. The Comedy of Job, *Semeia* 7:1.

White, E. B. 1979. Introduction, *Onward and Upward in the Garden*, by Katherine S. White. Boston: Beacon Press.

Wilde, Oscar. n/d. http://www.quotationspage.com (accessed 2007).

Willimon, William H., compiler. 1986. *And the Laugh Shall be First: A Treasury of Religious Humor*. Nashville: Abingdon Press.

———. 1994. *Leadership Journal* (Summer).

Yaconelli, Mike. 1989. It's Time to Party, *The Wittenburg Door* (May–June): 40.

———. 1998. *Dangerous Wonder*. Colorado Springs, Colo.: Navpress.